WHEN
GOD
WHISPERS
YOUR
NAME

WHEN GOD WHISPERS YOUR NAME

MAX LUCADO

WORD PUBLISHING
Nelson Word Ltd
Milton Keynes, England

WORD AUSTRALIA
Kilsyth, Australia

NELSON WORD CANADA
Vancouver, B.C., Canada

STRUIK CHRISTIAN BOOKS (PTY) LTD
Cape Town, South Africa

JOINT DISTRIBUTORS SINGAPORE –
ALBY COMMERCIAL ENTERPRISES PTE LTD
and
CAMPUS CRUSADE, ASIA LTD

PHILIPPINE CAMPUS CRUSADE FOR CHRIST
Quezon City, Philippines

CHRISTIAN MARKETING NEW ZEALAND LTD
Havelock North, New Zealand

JENSCO LTD
Hong Kong

SALVATION BOOK CENTRE
Malaysia

WHEN GOD WHISPERS YOUR NAME

First published by Word Incorporated, Dallas, Texas

First Uk edition Nelson Word Ltd, Milton Keynes 1994

ISBN 0-85009-692-8

Unless otherwise indicated, all Scripture references are from the New Century Version of the Bible, copyright © 1987, 1988, 1991, Word Publishing. Other Scripture quotations are from:

The New King James Version (NKJV), copyright © 1979, 1980, 1982, Thomas Nelson, Inc., Publisher. Used by permission.

The Holy Bible, New International Version (NIV), copyright © 1973, 1978, 1984, International Bible Society. Used by permission of Zondervan Bible Publishers.

The Living Bible (TLB), copyright © 1971 by Tyndale House Publishers, Wheaton, Ill. Used by permission.

The New Testament in Modern English by J. B. Phillips (PHILLIPS), published by The Macmillan Company, © 1958, 1960, 1972 by J. B. Phillips.

The Good News Bible, the Bible in Today's English Version (TEV). Old Testament, © 1976 American Bible Society. New Testament, © 1966, 1971, 1976, American Bible Society. Used by permission.

The Message, The New Testament in Contemporary English (THE MESSAGE) published by Nav Press, © 1993 by Eugene H. Peterson.

Reproduced, printed and bound in Great Britian for Nelson Word Ltd. by Cox and Wyman Ltd., Reading.

94 95 96 97 / 10 9 8 7 6 5 4 3 2

CONTENTS

Denalyn and I would like to dedicate this book to our *alma mater*—Abilene Christian University. We salute the board, administration, faculty, and staff. For all you've done and all you do, we applaud you.

So my dear brothers and sisters, stand strong. Do not let anything change you. Always give yourself fully to the work of the Lord, because you know your work in the Lord is never wasted.

1 Corinthians 15:58

ACKNOWLEDGEMENTS

The following people provided the necessary urgings, reminders, compliments, and kicks in the seat of my pants to get this job done.

Thanks to:

Karen Hill, my assistant. You know what I need before I ask for it. You know where it is when I've lost it. You know what it needs when I can't fix it. Are you human or angel?

Liz Heaney, my editor. Here's a toast to good books, long hours, and finished manuscripts. Thanks for another great job.

The Nelson Word family. Every single one of you. I'm honoured to be your partner.

To Steve and Cheryl Green. For your dedication to 'UpWords' and your loyal friendship.

To Steve Halliday, for writing the discussion guide.

To Terry Olivarri, for lessons on enjoying life.

To Jim Martin, a fine physician. A dear friend.

To my wife Denalyn. I'm having second thoughts about us.
Every second I have a thought about how grateful I am for
you.

And to you, the reader, may the words of this book guide you
to one Word which matters. His.

MAX LUCADO

INTRODUCTION

The sheep listen to the voice of the shepherd. He calls his own sheep by name and leads them out.

John 10:3

When I see a flock of sheep I see exactly that, a flock. A rabble of wool. A herd of hooves. I don't see *a* sheep. I see sheep. All alike. None different. That's what I see.

But not so with the shepherd. To him every sheep is different. Every face is special. Every face has a story. And every sheep has a name. *The one with the sad eyes, that's Droopy. And the fellow with one ear up and the other down, I call him Oscar. And the small one with the black patch on his leg, he's an orphan with no brothers. I call him Joseph.*

The shepherd knows his sheep. He calls them by name.

When we see a crowd, we see exactly that, a crowd. Filling a stadium or flooding a mall. When we see a crowd, we see people, not persons, but people. A herd of humans. A flock of faces. That's what we see.

But not so with the Shepherd. To Him every face is different. Every face is a story. Every face is a child. Every child has a name. *The one with the sad eyes, that's Sally. The old fellow with one eyebrow up and the other down, Harry's his name. And the young one with the limp? He's an orphan with no brothers. I call him Joey.*

The Shepherd knows His sheep. He knows each one by name. The Shepherd knows you. He knows your name. And

He will never forget it. *I have written your name on my hand* (Isa. 49:16).

Quite a thought, isn't it? Your name on God's hand. Your name on God's lips. Maybe you've seen your name in some special places. On an award or diploma or walnut door. Or maybe you've heard your name from some important people—a coach, a celebrity, a teacher. But to think that your name is on God's hand and on God's lips . . . my, could it be?

Or perhaps you've never seen your name honoured. And you can't remember when you heard it spoken with kindness. If so, it may be more difficult for you to believe that God knows your name.

But He does. Written on His hand. Spoken by His mouth. Whispered by His lips. Your name. And not only the name you now have, but the name He has in store for you. A new name He will give you . . . but wait, I'm getting ahead of myself. I'll tell you about your new name in the last chapter. This is just the introduction.

And so may I introduce you to this book? It's a book of hope. A book whose sole aim is to encourage. For the last year I've harvested thoughts from a landscape of fields. And though their size and flavours are varied, their purpose is singular: to provide you, the reader, with a word of hope. I thought you could use it.

You've been on my mind as I've been writing. I've thought of you often. I honestly have. Over the years I've got to know some of you folks well. I've read your letters, shaken your hands, and watched your eyes. I think I know you.

You're busy. Time passes before your tasks are finished. And if you get a chance to read, it's a slim chance indeed.

You're anxious. Bad news outpaces the good. Problems outnumber solutions. And you are concerned. What future do your children have on this earth? What future do you have?

You're cautious. You don't trust as easily as you once did.

Politicians lied. The system failed. The minister compromised. Your spouse cheated. It's not easy to trust. It's not that you don't want to. It's just that you want to be careful.

There is one other thing. You've made some mistakes. I met one of you at a bookstore in Michigan. A businessman, you seldom came out of your office at all and never to meet an author. But then you did. You were regretting the many hours at work and the few hours at home and wanted to talk.

And the single mum in Chicago. One kid was tugging, the other crying, but juggling them both, you made your point. 'I made mistakes,' you explained, 'but I really want to try again.'

And there was that night in Fresno. The musician sang and I spoke and you came. You almost didn't. You almost stayed home. Just that day you'd found the note from your wife. She was leaving you. But you came anyway. Hoping I'd have something for the pain. Hoping I'd have an answer. Where is God at a time like this?

And so as I wrote, I thought about you. All of you. You aren't malicious. You aren't evil. You aren't hardhearted (hardheaded occasionally, but not hardhearted). You really want to do what is right. But sometimes life turns sour. Occasionally we need a reminder.

Not a sermon.
A reminder.
A reminder that God knows your name.

Many chapters auditioned for this book, but not all were

selected. After all, not just any chapter would do. Brevity was required, for you are busy. Hope was needed, for you are anxious. Loyalty to Scripture was a mandate, for you are cautious. I sought to give you a repertoire of chapters that recite well the lyrics of grace and sing well the melody of joy. For you are the guest of the Maestro, and he is preparing a concert you'll never forget.

PART ONE

The Song
of the Minstrel

y wife loves antiques. I don't. (I find them a bit old.) But because I love my wife, I occasionally find myself guiding three children through an antique store while Denalyn shops. Such is the price of love.

The secret to survival in a shop of relics is to find a chair and an old book and settle down for the long haul. That's what I did yesterday. After cautioning the kids to look with their eyes and not with their hands, I sat down in an overstuffed rocker with some Life magazines from the fifties.

That's when I heard the music. Piano music. Beautiful music. Vintage Rogers and Hammerstein. The hills were alive with the sound of someone's skill at the keyboard.

I turned to see who was playing, but couldn't see anyone. I stood and walked closer. A small group of listeners had gathered at the old upright piano. Between the furniture I could see the small back of the pianist. Why, it's only a child! With a few more steps I could see her hair. Short, blonde, and cute like . . . My heart, it's Andrea!

Our seven-year-old was at the piano, her hands racing up and down the keyboard. I was stunned. What gift of heaven is this that she can play in such a way? Must be a time-released gene she got from my side of the family. But as I drew closer, I saw the real reason. Andrea was 'playing' a player piano. She wasn't making the music; she was following it. She wasn't commanding the keyboard; she was trying to keep up with it. Though it appeared she was playing the song, in reality, she was only trying to keep up with one already written. When a key would dip, her hands would dash.

*Oh, but if you could have seen her little face, delighted
with laughter! Eyes dancing as would her feet had she been
able to stand and play at the same time.*

I could see why she was so happy. She sat down to at-
tempt 'Chopsticks' but instead played 'The Sound of Music.'
What's more, she couldn't fail. One greater than she was
dictating the sound. Andrea was free to play as much as she
wanted, knowing the music would never suffer.

It's no wonder she rejoiced. She had every reason to. And
so do we.

Hasn't God promised the same to us? We sit at the
keyboard, willing to play the only song we know, only to discover a new song. A sublime song. And nobody is more surprised than we are when our meagre efforts are converted
into melodious moments.

You have one, you know, a song all your own. Each of us
does. The only question is, will you play it?

By the way, as I watched Andrea 'play' that day in the
antique store I observed a couple of things.

I noticed the piano got all the credit. The gathered crowd
appreciated Andrea's efforts, but they knew the real source of
the music. When God works, the same is true. We may applaud the disciple, but no one knows better than the disciple
who really deserves the praise.

But that doesn't keep the disciple from sitting at the
bench. It certainly didn't keep Andrea from sitting at the
piano. Why? Because she knew she couldn't fail. Even though
she didn't understand how it worked, she knew it did.

So she sat at the keyboard—and had the time of her life.

Even though you may not understand how God works,
you know He does.

So go ahead. Pull up a bench, take your seat at the piano,
and play.

CHAPTER ONE

The Voice from the Mop Bucket

The hallway is silent except for the wheels of the mop bucket and the shuffle of the old man's feet. Both sound tired.

Both know these floors. How many nights has Hank cleaned them? Always careful to get in the corners. Always careful to set up his yellow caution sign warning of wet floors. Always chuckling as he does. 'Be careful everyone,' he laughs to himself, knowing no one is near.

Not at three a.m.

Hank's health isn't what it used to be. Gout keeps him awake. Arthritis makes him limp. His glasses are so thick his eyeballs look twice their size. Shoulders stoop. But he does his work. Slopping soapy water on linoleum. Scrubbing the heel marks left by the well-heeled lawyers. He'll be finished an hour before quitting time. Always finishes early. Has for twenty years.

When finished he'll put away his bucket and take a seat outside the office of the senior partner and wait. Never leaves early. Could. No one would know. But he doesn't.

He broke the rules once. Never again.

Sometimes, if the door is open, he'll enter the office. Not

for long. Just to look. The suite is larger than his apartment. He'll run his finger over the desk. He'll stroke the soft leather couch. He'll stand at the window and watch the grey sky turn gold. And he'll remember.

He once had such an office.

Back when Hank was Henry. Back when the custodian was an executive. Long ago. Before the night shift. Before the mop bucket. Before the maintenance uniform. Before the scandal.

Hank doesn't think about it much now. No reason to. Got in trouble, got fired, and got out. That's it. Not many people know about it. Better that way. No need to tell them.

It's his secret.

Hank's story, by the way, is true. I changed the name and a detail or two. I gave him a different job and put him in a different century. But the story is factual. You've heard it. You know it. When I give you his real name, you'll remember.

But more than a true story, it's a common story. It's a story of a derailed dream. It's a story of high hopes colliding with harsh realities.

Happens to all dreamers. And since all have dreamed, it happens to us all.

In Hank's case, it was a mistake he could never forget. A grave mistake. Hank killed someone. He came upon a thug beating up an innocent man, and Hank lost control. He killed the mugger. When word got out, Hank got out.

Hank would rather hide than go to jail. So he ran. The executive became a fugitive.

True story. Common story. Most stories aren't as extreme as Hank's. Few spend their lives running from the law. Many, however, live with regrets.

'I could have gone to college on a golf scholarship,' a fellow told me just last week on the fourth tee box. 'Had an offer right out of school. But I joined a rock-and-roll band.

Ended up never going. Now I'm stuck fixing garage doors.'

'Now I'm stuck.' Epitaph of a derailed dream.

Pick up a high school yearbook and read the 'What I want to do' sentence under each picture. You'll get dizzy breathing the thin air of mountaintop visions:

> 'Ivy league school.'
> 'Write books and live in Switzerland.'
> 'Physician in a Third World country.'
> 'Teach inner-city kids.'

Yet, take the yearbook to a twentieth-year reunion and read the next chapter. Some dreams have come true, but many haven't. Not that all should, mind you. I hope the little guy who dreamed of being a sumo wrestler came to his senses. And I hope he didn't lose his passion in the process. Changing direction in life is not tragic. Losing passion in life is.

Something happens to us along the way. Convictions to change the world downgrade to commitments to pay the bills. Rather than make a difference, we make a salary. Rather than look forward, we look back. Rather than look outward, we look inward.

And we don't like what we see.

Hank didn't. Hank saw a man who'd settled for the mediocre. Trained in the finest institutions of the world, yet working the night shift in a minimum-wage job so he wouldn't be seen in the day.

But all that changed when he heard the voice from the mop bucket. (Did I mention that his story is true?)

At first he thought the voice was a joke. Some of the fellows on the third floor play these kinds of tricks.

'Henry, Henry,' the voice called.

Hank turned. No one called him Henry any more.

'Henry, Henry.'

He turned toward the pail. It was glowing. Bright red. Hot red. He could feel the heat ten feet away. He stepped closer and looked in. The water wasn't boiling.

'This is strange,' Hank mumbled to himself as he took another step to get a closer look. But the voice stopped him.

'Don't come any closer. Take off your shoes. You are on holy tile.'

Suddenly Hank knew who was speaking. 'God?'

I'm not making this up. I know you think I am. Sounds crazy. Almost irreverent. God speaking from a hot mop bucket to a janitor named Hank? Would it be believable if I said God was speaking from a burning bush to a shepherd named Moses?

Maybe that one's easier to handle—because you've heard it before. But just because it's Moses and a bush rather than Hank and a bucket, it's no less spectacular.

It shocked the sandals off Moses all right. We wonder what amazed the old fellow more: that God spoke in a bush or that God spoke at all.

Moses, like Hank, had made a mistake.

You remember his story. Adopted nobility. An Israelite reared in an Egyptian palace. His countrymen were slaves, but Moses was privileged. Ate at the royal table. Educated in the finest schools.

But his most influential teacher had no degree. She was his mother. A Jewess who was hired to be his nanny. 'Moses,' you can almost hear her whisper to her young son, 'God has put you here on purpose. Someday you will set your people free. Never forget, Moses. Never forget.'

Moses didn't. The flame of justice grew hotter until it blazed. Moses saw an Egyptian beating a Hebrew slave. Just like Hank killed the mugger, Moses killed the Egyptian.

The next day Moses saw the Hebrew. You'd think the slave would say thanks. He didn't. Rather than express gratitude, he expressed anger. 'Will you kill me too?' he asked (see Exod. 2:14).

Moses knew he was in trouble. He fled Egypt and hid in the wilderness. Call it a career shift. He went from dining with the heads of state to counting heads of sheep.

Hardly an upward move.

And so it happened that a bright, promising Hebrew began herding sheep in the hills. From the Ivy League to the cotton patch. From the Oval Office to a taxicab. From swinging a golf club to digging a ditch.

Moses thought the move was permanent. There is no indication he ever intended to go back to Egypt. In fact, there is every indication he wanted to stay with his sheep. Standing barefoot before the bush, he confessed, 'I am not a great man! How can I go to the king and lead the Israelites out of Egypt?' (Exod. 3:11).

I'm glad Moses asked that question. It's a good one. Why Moses? Or, more specifically, why eighty-year-old Moses?

The forty-year-old version was more appealing. The Moses we saw in Egypt was brash and confident. But the Moses we find four decades later is reluctant and weather-beaten.

Had you or I looked at Moses back in Egypt, we would have said, 'This man is ready for battle.' Educated in the finest system in the world. Trained by the ablest soldiers. Instant access to the inner circle of the Pharaoh. Moses spoke their language and knew their habits. He was the perfect man for the job.

Moses at forty we like. But Moses at eighty? No way. Too old. Too tired. Smells like a shepherd. Speaks like a foreigner. What impact would he have on Pharaoh? He's the wrong man for the job.

And Moses would have agreed. 'Tried that once before,' he would say. 'Those people don't want to be helped. Just leave me here to tend my sheep. They're easier to lead.'

Moses wouldn't have gone. You wouldn't have sent him. I wouldn't have sent him.

But God did. How do you figure? Benched at forty and suited up at eighty. Why? What does he know now that he didn't know then? What did he learn in the desert that he didn't learn in Egypt?

The ways of the desert, for one. Forty-year-old Moses was a city boy. Octogenarian Moses knows the name of every snake and the location of every watering hole. If he's going to lead thousands of Hebrews into the wilderness, he'd better know the basics of desert life.

Family dynamics, for another. If he's going to be travelling with families for forty years, it might help to understand how they work. He marries a woman of faith, the daughter of a Midianite priest, and establishes his own family.

But more than the ways of the desert and the people, Moses needed to learn something about himself.

Apparently he has learned it. God says Moses is ready.

And to convince him, God speaks through a bush. (Had to do something dramatic to get Moses' attention.)

'School's out,' God tells him. 'Now it's time to get to work.' Poor Moses. He didn't even know he was enrolled.

But he was. And, guess what. So are you. The voice from the bush is the voice that whispers to you. It reminds you that God is not finished with you yet. Oh, you may think He is. You may think you've peaked. You may think He's got someone else to do the job.

If so, think again.

'God began doing a good work in you, and I am sure He will continue it until it is finished when Jesus Christ comes again.'[1]

Did you see what God is doing? *A good work in you.*

Did you see when He will be finished? *When Jesus comes again.*

May I spell out the message? *God ain't finished with you yet.*

Your Father wants you to know that. And to convince you, He may surprise you. He may speak through a bush, a mop bucket, or stranger still, He may speak through this book.

CHAPTER TWO

Why Jesus Went to Parties

I was planning to write a chapter on twelve verses this week, but I never got past the second verse. Not supposed to do that. Supposed to present the entire story. I meant to, I really did. But I got stuck. The second verse wouldn't release me—it took me hostage—so I spent the whole lesson on one verse. Captivating little phrase, it was.

I'll tell you about it, after I set the stage.

Picture six men walking on a narrow road. The gold dawn explodes behind them, stretching shadows ahead. Early-morning chill has robes snugly wrapped. Grass sparkles with diamonds of dew.

The men's faces are eager, but common. Their leader is confident, but unknown. They call him Rabbi; he looks more like a labourer. And well he should, for he's spent far more time building than teaching. But this week the teaching has begun.

Where are they going? To the temple to worship? To the synagogue to teach? To the hills to pray? They haven't been told, but they each have their own idea.

John and Andrew expect to be led into the desert. That's

where their previous teacher had taken them. John the Baptist would guide them into the barren hills and for hours they would pray. For days they would fast. For the Messiah they would yearn. And now, the Messiah is here.

Surely He will do the same.

Everybody knows that a Messiah is a holy man. Everybody knows that self-denial is the first step to holiness. Surely God's voice is first heard by hermits. *Jesus is leading us into solitude.* At least that's what John and Andrew think.

Peter has another opinion. Peter is a man of action. A roll-up-your-sleeves kind of guy. A stand-up-and-say-it sort of fellow. He likes the idea of going somewhere. God's people need to be on the move. *Probably taking us somewhere to preach,* he is thinking to himself. And as they walk, Peter is outlining his own sermon, should Jesus need a breather.

Nathanael would disagree. *Come and see,* his friend Philip had invited. So he came. And Nathanael liked what he saw. In Jesus he saw a man of deep thought. A man of meditation. A heart of contemplation. A man who, like Nathanael, had spent hours under the fig tree reflecting on the mysteries of life. Nathanael was convinced that Jesus was taking them to a place to ponder. *A quiet house on a distant mountain, that's where we are going.*

And what about Philip? What was he thinking? He was the only apostle with a Gentile name. When the Greeks came looking for Jesus, it was Philip they approached. Perhaps he had Greek connections. Maybe Philip had a heart for Gentiles. If so, he was hoping this journey was a missionary one—out of Galilee. Out of Judea. Into a distant land.

Did such speculation occur? Who knows? I know it does today.

I know Jesus' followers often enlist with high aspirations and expectations. Disciples step in line with unspoken yet heartfelt agendas. Lips posed to preach to thousands. Eyes fixed on foreign shores. *I know where Jesus will take me,* the young disciples claim, and so they, like the first five, follow.

And they, like the first five, are surprised.

Maybe it was Andrew who asked it. Perhaps Peter. Could be that all approached Jesus. But I wager that at some point in the journey, the disciples expressed their assumptions.

'So Rabbi, where are You taking us? To the desert?'

'No,' opines another, 'He's taking us to the temple.'

'To the temple?' challenges a third. 'We're on our way to the Gentiles!'

Then a chorus of confusion breaks out and ends only when Jesus lifts His hand and says softly, 'We're on our way to a wedding.'

Silence. John and Andrew look at each other. 'A wedding?' they say. 'John the Baptist would have never gone to a wedding. Why, there is drinking and laughter and dancing . . .'

'And noise!' Philip chimes in. 'How can you meditate in a noisy wedding?'

'Or preach in a wedding?' Peter adds.

'Why would we go to a wedding?'

Good question. Why would Jesus, on His first journey, take His followers to a party? Didn't they have work to do? Didn't He have principles to teach? Wasn't His time limited? How could a wedding fit with His purpose on earth?

Why did Jesus go to the wedding?

The answer? It's found in the second verse of John 2 (the verse I could not pass). 'Jesus and his followers were also invited to the wedding.'

When the bride and groom were putting the guest list together, Jesus' name was included. And when Jesus showed up with half a dozen friends, the invitation wasn't rescinded. Whoever was hosting this party was happy to have Jesus present.

'Be sure and put Jesus' name on the list,' he might have said. 'He really lightens up a party.'

Jesus wasn't invited because He was a celebrity. He wasn't one yet. The invitation wasn't motivated by His miracles. He'd yet to perform any. Why did they invite Him?

I suppose they liked Him.

Big deal? I think so. I think it's significant that common folk in a little town enjoyed being with Jesus. I think it's noteworthy that the Almighty didn't act high and mighty. The Holy One wasn't holier-than-thou. The One who knew it all wasn't a know-all. The One who made the stars didn't keep His head in them. The One who owns all the stuff of earth never strutted it.

Never. He could have. Oh, how He could have!

He could have been a name-dropper: *Did I ever tell you of the time Moses and I went up on the mountain?'*

He could have been a show-off: *Hey, want me to beam you into the twentieth century?'*

He could have been a smart-aleck: *I know what you're thinking. Want me to prove it?'*

He could have been highbrow and uppity: *I've got some property on Jupiter . . .*

Jesus could have been all of these, but He wasn't. His purpose was not to show off but to show up. He went to great pains to be as human as the guy down the street. He didn't need to study, but still went to the synagogue. He had no need for income, but still worked in the workshop. He had known the fellowship of angels and heard the harps of heaven, yet still went to parties thrown by tax collectors. And upon His shoulders rested the challenge of redeeming creation, but He still took time to walk ninety miles from Jericho to Cana to go to a wedding.

As a result, people liked Him. Oh, there were those who chaffed at His claims. They called Him a blasphemer, but they never called Him a braggart. They accused Him of heresy, but never arrogance. He was branded as a radical, but never called unapproachable.

There is no hint that He ever used His heavenly status for personal gain. Ever. You just don't get the impression that His neighbours grew sick of His haughtiness and asked, 'Well, who do you think made you God?'

His faith made him likeable, not detestable. Would that ours would do the same!

Where did we get the notion that a good Christian is a solemn Christian? Who started the rumour that the sign of a disciple is a long face? How did we create this idea that the truly gifted are the heavy-hearted?

May I state an opinion that may raise an eyebrow? May I tell you why I think Jesus went to the wedding? I think He went to the wedding to—now hold on, hear me out, let me say it before you heat the tar and pluck the feathers—I think Jesus went to the wedding to have fun.

Think about it. It's been a tough season. Forty days in the desert. No food or water. A confrontation with the devil. A week breaking in some greenhorn Galileans. A job change. He's left home. It hasn't been easy. A break would be welcome. Good meal with some good wine and some good friends . . . well, it sounds pretty nice.

So off they go.

His purpose wasn't to turn the water to wine. That was a favour for His friends.

His purpose wasn't to show His power. The wedding host didn't even know what Jesus did.

His purpose wasn't to preach. There is no record of a sermon.

Really leaves only one reason. Fun. Jesus went to the wedding because He liked the people, He liked the food, and heaven forbid, He may have even wanted to swirl the bride around the dance floor a time or two. (After all, He's planning a big wedding Himself. Maybe He wanted the practice?)

So, forgive me, Deacon Drydust and Sister Sombreheart. I'm sorry to rain on your dirge, but Jesus was a likeable fellow. And His disciples should be the same. I'm not talking debauchery, drunkenness, and adultery. I'm not endorsing compromise, coarseness, or obscenity. I am simply crusading for the freedom to enjoy a good joke, enliven a dull party, and appreciate a fun evening.

Maybe these thoughts catch you by surprise. They do me. It's been a while since I pegged Jesus as a party-lover. But He was. His foes accused him of eating too much, drinking too much, and hanging out with the wrong people! (See Matt. 11:19.) I must confess: it's been a while since I've been accused of having too much fun. How about you?

We used to be good at it. What has happened to us? What happened to clean joy and loud laughter? Is it our buttoned collars and ties that choke us? Is it our diplomas that dignify us? Is it the pew that stiffens us?

Couldn't we learn to be children again?

Bring out the marbles—(so what if the shoes get scuffed?).

Bring out the bat and glove—(so what if the muscles ache?).

Bring out the toffee—(so what if it sticks to your teeth?).

Be a child again. Flirt. Giggle. Dip your cookie in your milk. Take a nap. Say you're sorry if you hurt someone. Chase a butterfly. Be a child again.

Loosen up. Don't you have some people to hug, rocks to skip, or lips to kiss? Someone needs to laugh at Bugs Bunny; might as well be you. Someday you're going to learn to paint; might as well be now. Someday you are going to retire; why not today?

Not retire from your job, just retire from your attitude. Honestly, has complaining ever made the day better? Has grumbling ever paid the bills? Has worrying about tomorrow ever changed it?

Let someone else run the world for a while.

Jesus took time for a party . . . shouldn't we?

CHAPTER THREE

Hidden Heroes

$\mathcal{T}$rue heroes are hard to identify. They don't look like heroes. Here's an example.

Step with me into a dank dungeon in Judea. Peer through the door's tiny window. Consider the plight of the man on the floor. He has just inaugurated history's greatest movement. His words have triggered a revolution that will span two millenniums. Future historians will describe him as courageous, noble, and visionary.

At this moment he appears anything but. Cheeks hollow. Beard matted. Bewilderment etched on his face. He leans back against the cold wall, closes his eyes, and sighs.

John had never known doubt. Hunger, yes. Loneliness, often. But doubt? Never. Only raw conviction, ruthless pronouncements, and rugged truth. Such was John the Baptist. Conviction as fierce as the desert sun.

Until now. Now the sun is blocked. Now his courage wanes. Now the clouds come. And now, as he faces death, he doesn't raise a fist of victory; he raises only a question. His final act is not a proclamation of courage, but a confession of confusion: 'Find out if Jesus is the Son of God or not.'

The forerunner of the Messiah is afraid of failure. *Find out if I've told the truth. Find out if I've sent people to the right Messiah. Find out if I've been right or if I've been duped.* [1]

Doesn't sound too heroic, does he?

We'd rather have John die in peace. We'd rather have the trailblazer catch a glimpse of the mountain. Seems only right that the sailor be granted a sighting of the shore. After all, didn't Moses get a view of the valley? Isn't John the cousin of Jesus? If anybody deserves to see the end of the trail, doesn't he?

Apparently not.

The miracles he prophesied, he never saw. The kingdom he announced, he never knew. And the Messiah he proclaimed, he now doubts.

John doesn't look like the prophet who would be the transition between law and grace. He doesn't look like a hero.

Heroes seldom do.

Can I take you to another prison for a second example?

This time the jail is in Rome. The man is named Paul. What John did to present Christ, Paul did to explain him. John cleared the path; Paul erected signposts.

Like John, Paul shaped history. And like John, Paul would die in the jail of a despot. No headlines announced his execution. No observer recorded the events. When the axe struck Paul's neck, society's eyes didn't blink. To them Paul was a peculiar purveyor of an odd faith.

Peer into the prison and see him for yourself: bent and frail, shackled to the arm of a Roman guard. Behold the apostle of God. Who knows when his back last felt a bed or his mouth knew a good meal? Three decades of travel and trouble, and what's he got to show for it?

There's squabbling in Philippi, competition in Corinth, the legalists are swarming in Galatia. Crete is plagued by money-grabbers. Ephesus is stalked by womanisers. Even some of Paul's own friends have turned against him.

Dead broke. No family. No property. Near-sighted and worn out.

Oh, he had his moments. Spoke to an emperor once, but couldn't convert him. Gave a lecture at an Areopagus men's club, but wasn't asked to speak there again. Spent a few days with Peter and the boys in Jerusalem, but they couldn't seem to get along, so Paul hit the road.

And never got off. Ephesus, Thessalonica, Athens, Syracuse, Malta. The only list longer than his itinerary was his misfortune. Got stoned in one city and stranded in another. Nearly drowned as many times as he nearly starved. If he spent more than one week in the same place, it was probably a prison.

He never received a salary. Had to pay his own travel expenses. Kept a part-time job on the side to make ends meet.

Doesn't look like a hero.

Doesn't sound like one either. He introduced himself as the worst sinner in history. He was a Christian-killer before he was a Christian leader. At times his heart was so heavy, Paul's pen dragged itself across the page. 'What a miserable man I am! Who will save me from this body that brings me death?' (Rom. 7:24).

Only heaven knows how long he stared at the question before he found the courage to defy logic and write, 'I thank God for saving me through Jesus Christ our Lord!' (Rom. 7:25).

One minute he's in charge; the next he's in doubt. One day he's preaching; the next he's in prison. And that's where I'd like you to look at him. Look at him in the prison.

Pretend you don't know him. You're a guard or a cook or a friend of the hatchet man, and you've come to get one last look at the guy while they sharpen the blade.

What you see shuffling around in his cell isn't too much. But what I lean over and tell you is: 'That man will shape the course of history.'

You chuckle, but I continue.

'Nero's fame will fade in this man's light.'

You turn and stare. I continue.

'His churches will die. But his thoughts? Within two hundred years his thoughts will influence the teaching of every school on this continent.'

You shake your head.

'See those letters? Those letters scribbled on parchment? They'll be read in thousands of languages and will impact every major creed and constitution of the future. Every major figure will read them. Every single one.'

That would be your breaking point. 'No way. He's an old man with an odd faith. He'll be killed and forgotten before his head hits the floor.'

Who could disagree? What rational thinker would counter?

Paul's name would blow away like the dust his bones would become.

Just like John's. No level-headed observer would think otherwise. Both were noble, but passing. Courageous, but small. Radical, yet unnoticed. No one—I repeat, no one—bade farewell to these men thinking their names would be remembered more than a generation.

Their peers simply had no way of knowing—and neither do we.

For that reason, a hero could be next door and you wouldn't know it. The fellow who changes the oil in your car could be one. A hero in overalls? Maybe. Maybe as he works he prays, asking God to do with the heart of the driver what he does with the engine.

The daycare worker where you drop off the kids? Perhaps. Perhaps her morning prayers include the name of each child and the dream that one of them will change the world. Who's to say God isn't listening?

The inner-city probation officer? Could be a hero. She could be the one who challenges the ex-con to challenge the teens to challenge the gangs.

I know, I know. These folks don't fit our image of a hero. They look too, too, . . . well, normal. Give us four stars, titles, and headlines. But something tells me that for every hero in the spotlight, there are dozens in the shadows. They don't get a press. They don't draw crowds. They don't even write books!

But behind every avalanche is a snowflake.

Behind a rock slide is a pebble.

An atomic explosion begins with one atom.

And a revival can begin with one sermon.

History proves it. John Egglen had never preached a sermon in his life. Never.

Wasn't that he didn't want to, just never needed to. But then one morning he did. The snow left his town of Colchester, England, buried in white. When he awoke on that January Sunday in 1850, he thought of staying home. Who would go to church in such weather?

But he reconsidered. He was, after all, a deacon. And if the deacons didn't go, who would? So he put on his boots, hat, and coat and walked the six miles to the Methodist Church.

He wasn't the only member who considered staying home. In fact, he was one of the few who came. Only thirteen people were present. Twelve members and one visitor. Even the minister was snowed in. Someone suggested they go home. Egglen would hear none of that. They'd come this far; they would have a service. Besides, they had a visitor. A thirteen-year-old boy.

But who would preach? Egglen was the only deacon. It fell to him.

And so he did. His sermon lasted only ten minutes. It drifted and wandered and made no point in an effort to make several. But at the end, an uncharacteristic courage settled upon the man. He lifted his eyes and looked straight at the boy and challenged: 'Young man, look to Jesus. Look! Look! Look!'

Did the challenge make a difference? Let the boy, now a man, answer. 'I did look, and then and there the cloud on my heart lifted, the darkness rolled away, and at that moment I saw the sun.'

The boy's name? Charles Haddon Spurgeon. England's prince of preachers.[2]

Did Egglen know what he'd done? No.

Do heroes know when they are heroic? Rarely.

Are historic moments acknowledged when they happen?

You know the answer to that one. (If not, a visit to the manger will remind you.) We seldom see history in the making, and we seldom recognise heroes. Which is just as well, for if we knew either, we might mess up both.

But we'd do well to keep our eyes open. Tomorrow's Spurgeon might be mowing your lawn. And the hero who inspires him might be nearer than you think.

He might be in your mirror.

CHAPTER FOUR

You Might've Been in the Bible

There are a few stories in the Bible where everything turns out right. This is one. It has three characters.

The first is Philip—a disciple in the early church who had a penchant for lost people. One day he was instructed by God to go to the road that leads to Gaza from Jerusalem. It was a desert road. He went. When he arrived he came upon a ruler from Ethiopia.

Must have been a bit intimidating for Philip. It would be similar to your hopping on a motor scooter and following the secretary of the treasury. At a stoplight you notice he is reading the Bible, and you volunteer your services.

That is what Philip did.

'Do you understand what you are reading?'

'How can I unless someone explains it to me?'

And so Philip did. They have a Bible study in the chariot. The study is so convicting that the Ethiopian is baptised that day. And then they separate. Philip goes one way, and the Ethiopian goes another. The story has a happy ending. Philip teaches, the Ethiopian obeys, and the gospel is sent to Africa.

But that's not all the story. Remember I said there were

three characters. The first was Philip; the second was the Ethiopian. Did you see the third? There is one. Read these verses and take note.

'An angel of the Lord said to Philip, "Get ready and go south. . . " So Philip got ready and went' (Acts 8: 26–27).

'The Spirit said to Philip, "Go to that chariot and stay near." So . . . Philip ran toward the chariot' (Acts 8: 29–30).

The third character? God! *God* sent the angel. The Holy Spirit instructed Philip; God orchestrated the entire moment! He saw this godly man coming from Ethiopia to worship. He saw his confusion. So he decided to resolve it.

He looked in Jerusalem for a man He could send. He found Philip.

Our typical response when we read these verses is to think Philip was a special guy. He had access to the Oval Office. He carried a first-century pager that God doesn't pass out any more.

But don't be too quick. In a letter to Christians just like us, Paul wrote, 'Live by following the Spirit' (Gal. 5:16).

'The true children of God are those who let God's Spirit lead them' (Rom. 8:14).

To hear many of us talk, you'd think we didn't believe these verses. You'd think we didn't believe in the Trinity. We talk about the Father and study the Son—but when it comes to the Holy Spirit, we are confused at best and frightened at worst. Confused because we've never been taught. Frightened because we've been taught to be afraid.

May I simplify things a bit? The Holy Spirit is the presence of God in our lives, carrying on the work of Jesus. The Holy Spirit helps us in three directions—inwardly (by granting us the fruits of the Spirit, Gal. 5:22–24), upwardly (by praying for us, Rom. 8:26) and outwardly (by pouring God's love into our hearts, Rom. 5:5).

In evangelism the Holy Spirit is on centre stage. If the disciple teaches, it is because the Spirit teaches the disciple (Luke 12:12). If the listener is convicted, it is because the Spirit has penetrated (John 16:10). If the listener is converted, it is by the transforming power of the Spirit (Rom. 8:11). If the new believer matures, it is because the Spirit makes him or her competent (2 Cor. 3:6).

You have the same Spirit working with you that Philip did. Some of you don't believe me. You're still cautious. I can hear you mumbling under your breath as you read, 'Philip had something I don't. I've never heard an angel's voice.' To which I counter, 'How do you know Philip did?'

We assume he did. We've been taught he did. The flannelboard figures say he did. An angel puts his trumpet in Philip's ear, blares the announcement, and Philip has no choice. Flashing lights and fluttering wings are nothing to deny. The deacon had to go. But could our assumption be wrong? Could it be that the angel's voice was every bit as miraculous as the one you and I hear?

What?

You've heard the voice whispering your name, haven't you? You've felt the nudge to go and sensed the urge to speak. Hasn't it occurred to you?

You invite a couple over for coffee. Nothing heroic, just a nice evening with old friends. But from the moment they enter, you can feel the tension. Colder than glaciers, they are. You can tell something is wrong. Typically you're not one to inquire, but you feel a concern that won't be silent. So you ask.

You are in a business meeting where one of your co-workers gets raked over the coals. Everyone else is thinking, *I'm glad that wasn't me.* But the Holy Spirit is leading you to think, *How hard this must be.* So, after the meeting you approach the employee and express your concern.

You notice the fellow on the other side of the church auditorium. He looks a bit out of place, what with his strange clothing and all. You learn that he is from Africa, in town on business. The next Sunday he is back. And the third Sunday he is present. You introduce yourself. He tells you how he is fascinated by the faith and how he wants to learn more. Rather than offer to teach him, you simply urge him to read the Bible.

Later in the week, you regret not being more direct. You call the office where he is consulting and learn that he is leaving today for home. You know in your heart you can't let him leave. So you rush to the airport and find him awaiting his flight, with a Bible open on his lap.

'Do you understand what you are reading?' you inquire.

'How can I, unless someone explains it to me?'

And so you, like Philip, explain. And he, like the Ethiopian, believes. Baptism is requested and baptism is offered. He catches a later flight and you catch a glimpse of what it means to be led by the Spirit.

Were there lights? You just lit one. Were there voices? You just were one. Was there a miracle? You just witnessed one. Who knows? If the Bible were being written today, that might be your name in the eighth chapter of Acts.

CHAPTER FIVE

Maxims

Here's a toast to the simple sentence.

Here's a salute to one-liners.

Join me in applauding the delete key and the eraser. May they feast on the trimmings of the writer's table.

I believe in brevity. Cut the fat and keep the fact. Give us words to chew on, not words to wade through. Thoughts that spark, not lines that drag. More periods. Fewer commas.

Distil it.

Barebone it.

Bareknuckle it.

Concise (but not cute). Clear (but not shallow). Vivid (but not detailed). That's good writing. That's good reading. But that's hard work!

But, it's what we like. We appreciate the chef who cuts the gristle before he serves the steak. We salute the communicator who does the same.

Ahhh, brevity. An art apparently unheeded in the realms of insurance brochures and some-assembly-required bicycle manuals.

We learn brevity from Jesus. His greatest sermon can be

read in eight minutes (Matthew 5—7). His best-known story can be read in ninety seconds (Luke 15:11–32). He summarised prayer in five phrases (Matt. 6:9–13). He silenced accusers with one challenge (John 8:7). He rescued a soul with one sentence (Luke 23:43). He summarised the Law in three verses (Mark 12:29–31), and He reduced all His teachings to one command (John 15:12).

He made His point and went home.

We preachers would do well to imitate. (What's that old line? 'Our speaker today needs no introduction, but he could use a conclusion.')

I believe in brevity. I believe that you, the reader, entrust me, the writer, with your most valued commodity—your time. I shouldn't take more than my share. For that reason, I love the short sentence. Big-time game it is. Hiding in the jungle of circular construction and six-syllable canyons. As I write, I hunt. And when I find, I shoot. Then I drag the treasure out of the trees and marvel.

Not all of my prey make their way into chapters. So what becomes of them? I save them. But I can't keep them to myself. So, may I invite you to see my trophy case? What follows are cuts from this book and a couple of others. Keep the ones you like. Forgive the ones you don't. Share them when you can. But if you do, keep it brief.

Pray all the time. If necessary, use words.
Sacrilege is to feel guilt for sins forgiven.
God forgets the past. Imitate Him.
Greed I've often regretted. Generosity—never.
Never miss a chance to read a child a story.
Pursue forgiveness, not innocence.
Be doubly kind to the people who bring your food or
    park your car.
In buying a gift for your wife, practicality can be

more expensive than extravagance.

Don't ask God to do what you want. Ask God to do what is right.

Nails didn't hold God to a cross. Love did.

You'll give up on yourself before God will.

Know answered prayer when you see it, and don't give up when you don't.

Flattery is fancy dishonesty.

The right heart with the wrong creed is better than the right creed with the wrong heart.

We treat others as we perceive God is treating us.

Sometimes the most godly thing we can do is take a day off.

Faith in the future begets power in the present.

No one is useless to God. No one.

Conflict is inevitable, but combat is optional.

You will never forgive anyone more than God has already forgiven you.

Succeed in what matters.

You'll regret opening your mouth. You'll rarely regret keeping it shut.

To see sin without grace is despair. To see grace without sin is arrogance. To see them in tandem is conversion.

Faith is the grit in the soul that puts the dare into dreams.

God doesn't keep a clock.

Never underestimate a gesture of affection.

When Jesus went home, He left the front door open.

And to sum it up:

As soon as you can, pay your debts.

As long as you can, give the benefit of the doubt.

As much as you can, give thanks. He's already given us more than we deserve.

CHAPTER SIX

God's Christmas Cards

I'm monitoring my mailbox.

I don't usually spend time looking at it, but I am today. I don't want it to fall. Just a few days ago that wasn't a concern—but that was before the construction crew started clearing the building site across the street. And that was before the gravel-truck driver forgot to look in his rear-view mirror.

Clunk.

So today our mailbox is upright again, propped up by three two-by-fours on three sides. Not too attractive, but functional.

Strange what you think about while posting an eye on the postal receptacle. As I gaze at it, it occurs to me that the mailbox is a lot like a bus terminus—a turnstile for the good and the bad, the wanted and the unwanted. Just for fun, I'm making a list of letters I hope I never receive. (Well, what do *you* think about when you're watching a box on a pole?)

Here's what I've written so far:

Dear Dad,
    I'm writing to ask if there is a limitation to the number of cars our insurance covers . . .

Dear Max,
    You know last summer when you broke the vase my Uncle Bill had left me? Remember I told you a hundred pounds would be fine, but you insisted I get it appraised? Well, boy, am I glad you did. I hope you are sitting down because the museum's curator of thirteenth-century art says . . .

Mr Lucado,
    The purpose of this letter is to inform you that the pure bred puppy you were sending to Oakland, California, was inadvertently sent to Auckland, New Zealand . . .

Dear Max,
    So why am I writing after all these years? Well, it seems that the university made a mistake. They swapped our papers. Isn't that a hoot? And all these years I thought I graduated by the skin of my teeth. And all these years you thought you were *summa cum laude*!

Dear Mrs Lucado,
    Recently you purchased from us a home pregnancy diagnostic kit. We are writing to inform you that there was a mistake in the instructions, and what you thought you were, you aren't, and what you thought you weren't, you are. . . .

Groan.

I've never read any scientific data on it, but it seems to me that the unnecessary mail has the necessary mail outnumbered. (Maybe you are like me and you sort your mail over a rubbish bin. Maybe you are like me and wonder if there is anything in the world that doesn't have its own catalogue. If you are a left-handed, right-winged, Ivy-League fan of jazz music, there is probably an underwear catalogue just for you.)

Most mail is unnecessary. So why am I repairing my box? Simple. It's December.

Were it any other time of the year, I might leave it on its side. Let the postman hang on to my bills for a few days. But I can't do that. Not this time of the year. Not December. Not the week before Christmas!

This is the week that mail is fun. This is the week of red envelopes, green stamps, and Christmas tree stickers. This is the week when your old roommate who married Hazel and moved to Phoenix writes to tell you their fourth child is on the way. This is the week of front-and-back newsletters describing the Grand Canyon, graduations, and gall-bladder surgeries.

This is the week of overnighted nuts and packaged fruit-cakes and frenzied postmen. Add to that a gift from Aunt Sophie and a calendar from your insurance agent, and you've got a daily reason to whistle your way to the mailbox.

So, as much for me as for the postman, I propped up the box.

Only a Scrooge doesn't want a Christmas card.

Some are funny. Got one today with elves pulling books off the 'elf-help' shelf.

Others are touching, like the illustration of Mother Mary and the baby resting at the base of the Egyptian sphinx.

And a few are unforgettable. Every Christmas I read this reminder that came in the post several years ago:

> *If our greatest need had been information, God would have sent an educator. If our greatest need had been technology, God would have sent us a scientist. If our greatest need had been money, God would have sent us an economist. But since our greatest need was forgiveness, God sent us a Saviour.*

Christmas cards. Punctuated promises. Phrases filled with the reason we do it all anyway.

> *He became like us, so we could become like Him. Angels still sing and the star still beckons. He loves each one of us as if there was only one of us to love.*

Long after the sender's name is forgotten, the card's message lingers. Words of promise. A handful of seeds and syllables flung upon the fertile soil of December with hope of fruit born in July. For that reason, I keep the mailbox up.

My heart can use all the seeds it can get.

CHAPTER SEVEN

Behind the
Shower Curtain

I'm going to have to install a computer in my shower. That's where I have my best thoughts.

I had a great one today.

I was mulling over a recent conversation I had with a disenchanted Christian brother. He was upset with me. So upset that he was considering rescinding his invitation for me to speak to his group. Seems he'd heard I was pretty open about who I have fellowship with. He'd read the words I wrote: 'If God calls a person His child, shouldn't I call him my brother?' And, 'If God accepts others with their errors and misinterpretations, shouldn't we?'[1]

He didn't like that. 'Carrying it a bit too far,' he told me. 'Fences are necessary,' he explained. 'Scriptures are clear on such matters.' He read me a few and then urged me to be careful to whom I give grace.

'I don't give it,' I assured. 'I only spotlight where God already has.'

Didn't seem to satisfy him. I offered to bow out of the engagement (the break would be nice), but he softened and told me to come after all.

That's where I'm going today. That's why I was thinking about him in the shower. And that's why I need a waterproof computer. I had a great thought. A why-didn't-I-think-to-say-that? insight.

I hope to see him today. If the subject resurfaces, I'll say it. But in case it doesn't, I'll say it to you. (It's too good to waste.) Just one sentence:

> I've never been surprised by God's judgement,
> but I'm still stunned by His grace.

God's judgement has never been a problem for me. In fact, it always seemed right. Lightning bolts on Sodom. Fire on Gomorrah. *Good job, God.* Egyptians swallowed in the Red Sea. *They had it coming.* Forty years of wandering to loosen the stiff necks of the Israelites? *Would've done it myself.* Ananias and Sapphira? *You bet.*

Discipline is easy for me to swallow. Logical to assimilate. Manageable and appropriate.

But God's grace? Anything but.

Examples? How much time do you have?

> David the psalmist becomes David the voyeur, but by God's grace becomes David the psalmist again.

> Peter denied Christ before he preached Christ.

> Zacchaeus, the crook. The cleanest part of his life was the money he'd laundered. But Jesus still had time for him.

> The thief on the cross: hellbent and hung-out-

to-die one minute, heaven-bound and smiling
the next.

Story after story. Prayer after prayer. Surprise after surprise.

Seems that God is looking more for ways to get us home than for ways to keep us out. I challenge you to find one soul who came to God seeking grace and did not find it. Search the pages. Read the stories. Envision the encounters. Find one person who came seeking a second chance and left with a stern lecture. I dare you. Search.

You won't find it.

You will find a strayed sheep on the other side of the creek. He's lost. He knows it. He's stuck and embarrassed. What will the other sheep say? What will the shepherd say?

You will find a shepherd who finds him. [2]

Oh boy. Duck down. Put hooves over the eyes. The belt is about to fly. But the belt is never felt. Just hands. Large, open hands reaching under his body and lifting the sheep up, up, up until he's placed upon the shepherd's shoulders. He's carried back to the flock and given a party! 'Cut the grass and comb the wool,' he announces. 'We are going to have a celebration!'

The other sheep shake their heads in disbelief. Just like we will. At our party. When we get home. When we watch the Shepherd shoulder into our midst one unlikely soul after another.

Seems to me God gives a lot more grace than we'd ever imagine.

We could do the same.

I'm not for watering down the truth or compromising the gospel. But if a fellow with a pure heart calls God *Father*, can't I call that same man *Brother*? If God doesn't make doctrinal perfection a requirement for family membership, should I?

And if we never agree, can't we agree to disagree? If God can tolerate my mistakes, can't I tolerate the mistakes of others? If God can overlook my errors, can't I overlook the errors of others? If God allows me with my foibles and failures to call Him *Father*, shouldn't I extend the same grace to others?

One thing's for sure. When we get to heaven, we'll be surprised at some of the folks we see. And some of them will be surprised when they see us.

CHAPTER EIGHT

Gabriel's Questions

Gabriel must have scratched his head at this one.

He wasn't one to question his God-given missions. Sending fire and dividing seas were all in an eternity's work for this angel. When God sent, Gabriel went.

And when word got out that God was to become man, Gabriel was enthused. He could envision the moment:

> The Messiah in a blazing chariot.
> The King descending on a fiery cloud.
> An explosion of light from which the Messiah would emerge.

That's what he expected. What he never expected, however, was what he got: a slip of paper with a Nazarene address. 'God will become a baby,' it read. 'Tell the mother to name the child Jesus. And tell her not to be afraid.'

Gabriel was never one to question, but this time he had to wonder.

God will become a baby? Gabriel had seen babies before. He had been platoon leader on the bulrush operation. He remembered what little Moses looked like.

That's OK for humans, he thought to himself. *But God?*

The heavens can't contain Him; how could a body? Besides, have you seen what comes out of those babies? Hardly befitting for the Creator of the universe. Babies must be carried and fed, bounced and bathed. To imagine some mother burping God on her shoulder—why, that was beyond what even an angel could imagine.

And what of this name—what was it—*Jesus?* Such a common name. There's a Jesus in every cul-de-sac. Come on, even *Gabriel* has more punch to it than *Jesus.* Call the baby *Eminence* or *Majesty* or *Heaven-sent.* Anything but *Jesus.*

So Gabriel scratched his head. What happened to the good ol' days? The Sodom and Gomorrah stuff. Flooding the globe. Flaming swords. That's the action he liked.

But Gabriel had his orders. Take the message to Mary. *Must be a special girl,* he assumed as he travelled. But Gabriel was in for another shock. One peek told him Mary was no queen. The mother-to-be of God was not regal. She was a Jewish peasant who'd barely outgrown her acne and had a crush on a guy named Joe.

And speaking of Joe—what does this fellow know? Might as well be a weaver in Spain or a cobbler in Greece. He's a carpenter. Look at him over there, sawdust in his beard and nail apron around his waist. You're telling me God is going to have dinner every night with him? You're telling me the source of wisdom is going to call this guy 'Dad?' You're telling me a common labourer is going to be charged with giving food to God?

What if he gets laid off?

What if he gets cranky?

What if he decides to run off with a pretty young girl from down the street? Then where will we be?

It was all Gabriel could do to keep from turning back.

'This is a peculiar idea you have, God,' he must have muttered to himself.

Are God's guardians given to such musings?

Are we? Are we still stunned by God's coming? Still staggered by the event? Does Christmas still spawn the same speechless wonder it did two thousand years ago?

I've been asking that question lately—to myself. As I write, Christmas is only days away and something just happened that has me concerned that the pace of the holidays may be overshadowing the purpose of the holidays.

I saw a manger in a shopping precinct. Correct that. I *barely* saw a manger in a shopping precinct. I almost didn't see it. I was in a hurry. Guests coming. Santa dropping in. Sermons to be prepared. Services to be planned. Presents to be purchased.

The crush of things was so great that the crèche of Christ was almost ignored. I nearly missed it. And had it not been for the child and his father, I would have.

But out of the corner of my eye, I saw them. The little boy, three, maybe four years old, in jeans and high-tops staring at the manger's infant. The father, in baseball hat and work clothes, looking over his son's shoulder, gesturing first at Joseph, then Mary, then the baby. He was telling the little fellow the story.

And oh, the twinkle in the boy's eyes. The wonder on his little face. He didn't speak. He just listened. And I didn't move. I just watched. What questions were filling the little boy's head? Could they have been the same as Gabriel's? What sparked the amazement on his face? Was it the magic?

And why is it that out of a hundred or so of God's children only two paused to consider His Son? What is this December demon that steals our eyes and stills our tongues?

Isn't this the season to pause and pose Gabriel's questions?

The tragedy is not that we can't answer them, but that we are too busy to ask them.

Only heaven knows how long Gabriel fluttered unseen above Mary before he took a breath and broke the news. But he did. He told her the name. He told her the plan. He told her not to be afraid. And when he announced, 'With God nothing is impossible!' he said it as much for himself as for her.

For even though he couldn't answer the questions, he knew who could, and that was enough. And even though we can't answer them all, taking time to ask a few would be a good start.

CHAPTER NINE

What Is Your Price?

*A*ttending an american game show wasn't your idea of a holiday activity, but your kids wanted to go, so you gave in. Now that you're here, you are beginning to enjoy it. The studio frenzy is contagious. The music is upbeat. The stage is colourful. And the stakes are high.

'Higher than they've ever been!' The show host brags. 'Welcome to *What Is Your Price?*' You're just about to ask your spouse if that is his real hair when he announces the pot: 'Ten million dollars!'

The audience needs no prompting; they explode with applause.

'It's the richest game in history,' the host beams. 'Someone today will walk out of here with a cheque for ten million!'

'Won't be me,' you chuckle to your oldest child. 'I've never had any luck at luck.'

'Shhhh,' she whispers, pointing to the stage. 'They're about to draw the name.'

Guess whose name they call. In the instant it takes to call it, you go from spectator to player. Your kids shriek, your spouse screams, and a thousand eyes watch the pretty girl take your hand and walk you to the stage.

'Open the curtain!' the host commands. You turn and watch as the curtains part and you gasp at the sight. A bright red wheelbarrow full of money—overflowing with money. The same girl who walked you to the stage now pushes the wheelbarrow in your direction, parking it in front of you.

'Ever seen ten million dollars?' asks the pearly-toothed host.

'Not in a while,' you answer. The audience laughs as if you were a stand-up comic.

'Dig your hands in it,' he invites. 'Go ahead, dive in.'

You look at your family. One child is drooling, one is praying, and your mate is giving you two thumbs up. How can you refuse? You burrow in up to your shoulders and rise up, clutching a chestful of one-hundred-dollar notes.

'It can be yours. It can be all yours. The choice is up to you. The only question you have to answer is, "What is your price?"'

Applause rings again, the band plays, and you swallow hard. Behind you a second curtain opens, revealing a large placard. 'What are you willing to give?' is written on the top. The host explains the rules. 'All you have to do is agree to one condition and you will receive the money.'

'Ten million dollars!' you whisper to yourself.

Not one million or two, but *ten* million. That must be about eight million pounds sterling. No small sum. Nice nest egg. Eight million pounds would go a long way, right? Tuition paid off. Retirement guaranteed. Would open a few doors on a few cars or a new house (or several).

You could be quite the benefactor with such a sum. Help a few orphanages. Feed a few nations. Build some church buildings. Suddenly you understand: this is the opportunity of a lifetime.

'Take your pick. Just choose one option and the money is yours.'

A deep voice from another microphone begins reading the list.

> 'Put your children up for adoption.'
> 'Become a prostitute for a week.'
> 'Give up your citizenship of your country.'
> 'Abandon your church.'
> 'Abandon your family.'
> 'Kill a stranger.'
> 'Have a sex-change operation.'
> 'Leave your spouse.'
> 'Change your race.'

'That's the list,' the host proclaims. 'Now make your choice.'

The theme music begins, the audience is quiet, and your pulse is racing. You have a choice to make. No one can help you. You are on the stage. The decision is yours. No one can tell you what to pick.

But there is one thing I can tell you. I can tell you what others would do. Your neighbours have given their answers. In a survey in the USA that asked the same question, many said what they would do. Seven per cent of those who answered would murder for the money. Six per cent would change their race. Four per cent would change their sex.[1]

If money is the gauge of the heart, then this study revealed that money is on the heart of most Americans. In exchange for ten million dollars:

> 25 per cent would abandon their family.
> 25 per cent would abandon their church.
> 23 per cent would become a prostitute for a week.

16 per cent would give up their American citizenship.

16 per cent would leave their spouse.

3 per cent would put their children up for adoption.[2]

Even more revealing than what Americans would do for ten million dollars is that most would do *something*. Two-thirds of those polled would agree to at least one—some to several—of the options. The majority, in other words, would not leave the stage empty-handed. They would pay the price to own the wheelbarrow.

What would you do? Or better, what are you doing?

'Get real, Max,' you are saying. 'I've never had a shot at ten million.'

Perhaps not, but you've had a chance to make a thousand or a hundred or ten. The amount may not have been the same but the choices are. Which makes the question even more disturbing. Some are willing to give up their family, faith, or morals for far less than ten million dollars.

Jesus had a word for that: *greed*.

Jesus also had a definition for greed. He called it the practice of measuring life by possessions.[3]

Greed equates a person's worth with a person's purse.

1. You got a lot = you are a lot.
2. You got a little = you are little.

The consequence of such a philosophy is predictable. If you are the sum of what you own, then by all means own it all. No price is too high. No payment is too much.

Now, very few would be guilty of blatant greed. Jesus knew that. That's why He cautioned against 'all kinds of greed' (Luke 12:15). Greed wears many faces.

When we lived in Rio de Janeiro, Brazil, I went to visit a member of our church. He had been a strong leader in the congregation, but for several Sundays we didn't see or hear from him.

Friends told me he had inherited some money and was building a house. I found him at the construction site. He'd inherited three hundred dollars. With the money he'd purchased a tiny lot adjacent to a polluted swamp. The plot of land was the size of a garage. On it he was, by hand, constructing a one-room house. He gave me a tour of the project—it took about twenty seconds.

We sat in front and talked. I told him we'd missed him, that the church needed him back. He grew quiet and turned and looked at his house. When he turned again his eyes were moist.

'You're right, Max,' he confessed. 'I guess I just got too greedy.'

Greedy? I wanted to say. *You're building a hut in a swamp and you call it greed?* But I didn't say anything because he was right. Greed is relative. Greed is not defined by what something costs; it is measured by what it costs you.

If anything costs you your faith or your family, the price is too high.

Such is the point Jesus makes in the parable of the portfolio.[4] Seems a fellow made a windfall profit off an investment. The land produced a bumper crop. He found himself with excess cash and an enviable question, 'What will I do with my earnings?'

Doesn't take him long to decide. He will save it. He will find a way to store it so he can live the good life. His plan? Accumulate. His aim? Wine, dine, shine, and recline. Move to the Sunbelt, play golf, kick back, and relax.

Suddenly, the man dies and another voice is heard. The voice of God. God has nothing kind to say to the man. His initial words are 'Foolish man!'

On earth the man was respected. He is honoured with a nice funeral and a mahogany coffin. Grey flannel suits fill the auditorium with admiration for the canny businessman. But on the front pew is a family already starting to bicker over their dad's estate. 'Foolish man!' God declares. 'So who will get those things you have prepared for yourself?' (Luke 12:20).

The man spent his life building a house of cards. He never saw the storm. And now, the wind has blown.

The storm wasn't the only thing he didn't see.

He never saw God. Note his first words after the capital gain. '*What will I do?*' (v. 17). He went to the wrong place and asked the wrong question. What if he'd gone to God and asked, 'What would You have me to do?'

The man's sin is not that he planned for the future. His sin was that his plans did not include God.

Imagine if someone treated you like this. Let's say you bring over a housesitter to care for your home over a weekend. You leave her with keys, money, and instructions. And you leave to enjoy your trip.

When you return, you find your house has been painted purple. The locks have been changed, so you ring the doorbell and the housesitter answers. Before you can say anything, she escorts you in proclaiming, 'Look how I decorated my house!'

The fireplace has been replaced with an indoor waterfall. Carpet has been replaced with pink tile, and portraits of Elvis on black velvet line the walls.

'This isn't your house!' you proclaim. 'It's mine.'

'Those aren't your possessions,' God reminds us. 'They are mine.'

'The LORD owns the world and everything in it—the heavens, even the highest heavens, are his' (Deut. 10:14).

God's foremost rule of finance is: we own nothing. We are managers, not owners. Stewards, not landlords. Maintenance people, not proprietors. Our money is not ours; it is His.

This man, however, gave no thought to that. Please note that Jesus didn't criticise this man's affluence. He criticised his arrogance. The rich man's words testify to his priority.

This is what I will do:
I will tear down . . .
I will store . . .
Then I can say to myself, 'I have enough good things.'
(Luke 12:18–19)

A schoolboy was once asked to define the parts of speech, *I* and *mine*. He answered, 'aggressive pronouns.' This rich man was aggressively self-centred. His world was fenced in by himself. He was blind. He didn't see God. He didn't see others. He saw only self.

'Foolish man,' God told him. 'Tonight your life will be taken from you' (v. 20).

Strange, isn't it, that this man had enough sense to acquire wealth but not enough to get ready for eternity? Stranger still, that we make the same mistake. I mean, it's not as if God kept the future a secret. One glance at a cemetery should remind us; everyone dies. One visit to a funeral should convince us; we don't take anything with us.

Hearses pull no trailers.

Dead men push no ten-million-dollar wheelbarrows.

The game show was pretend, but the facts are real. You are on a stage. You have been given a prize. The stakes are high. Very high.

What is your price?

CHAPTER TEN

Groceries and Grace

This story made its way to me from a friend who heard it from a friend who heard it from who knows who. Chances are it has suffered through each of the generations—but even if there is only a splinter of fact in what I heard, it's worth retelling.

Seems a fellow is doing some shopping at a commissary* on a military base. Doesn't need much, just some coffee and a loaf of bread. He is standing in line at the checkout stand. Behind him is a woman with a full trolley Her basket overflows with groceries, clothing, and a VCR.

At his turn he steps up to the register. The clerk invites him to draw a piece of paper out of a fishbowl. 'If you pull out the correct slip, then all your groceries are free,' the clerk explains.

'How many "correct slips" are there?' asks the buyer.

'Only one.'

The bowl is full so the chances are slim, but the fellow tries anyway, and wouldn't you know it, he gets the winning

---

*Shop on a US military base

ticket! What a surprise. But then he realises he is only buying coffee and bread. What a waste.

But this fellow is quick. He turns to the lady behind him—the one with the mountain of stuff—and proclaims, 'Well, what do you know, Honey? We won! We don't have to pay a penny.'

She stares at him. He winks at her. And somehow she has the wherewithal to play along. She steps up beside him. Puts her arm in his and smiles. And for a moment they stand side-by-side, wedded by good fortune. In the car park she consummates the temporary union with a kiss and a hug and goes on her way with a grand story to tell her friends.

I know, I know. What they did was a bit shady. He shouldn't have lied and she shouldn't have pretended. But that taken into account, it's still a nice story.

A story not too distant from our own. We, too, have been graced with a surprise. Even more than that of the lady. For though her debt was high, she could pay it. We can't begin to pay ours.

We, like the woman, have been given a gift. Not just at the checkout stand, but at the judgement seat.

And we, too, have become a bride. Not just for a moment, but for eternity. And not just for groceries, but for the feast.

Don't we have a grand story to tell our friends?

CHAPTER ELEVEN

The Choice

It's quiet. It's early. My coffee is hot. The sky is still black. The world is still asleep. The day is coming.

In a few moments the day will arrive. It will roar down the track with the rising of the sun. The stillness of the dawn will be exchanged for the noise of the day. The calm of solitude will be replaced by the pounding pace of the human race. The refuge of the early morning will be invaded by decisions to be made and deadlines to be met.

For the next twelve hours I will be exposed to the day's demands. It is now that I must make a choice. Because of Calvary, I'm free to choose. And so I choose.

I choose love . . .

No occasion justifies hatred; no injustice warrants bitterness. I choose love. Today I will love God and what God loves.

I choose joy . . .

I will invite my God to be the God of circumstance. I will refuse the temptation to be cynical . . . the tool of the lazy thinker. I will refuse to see people as anything less than human beings, created by God. I will refuse to see any problem as anything less than an opportunity to see God.

I choose peace . . .

I will live forgiven. I will forgive so that I may live.

I choose patience . . .

I will overlook the inconveniences of the world. Instead of cursing the one who takes my place, I'll invite him to do so. Rather than complain that the wait is too long, I will thank God for a moment to pray. Instead of clenching my fist at new assignments, I will face them with joy and courage.

I choose kindness . . .

I will be kind to the poor, for they are alone. Kind to the rich, for they are afraid. And kind to the unkind, for such is how God has treated me.

I choose goodness . . .

I will go without before I take dishonest gain. I will be overlooked before I will boast. I will confess before I will accuse. I choose goodness.

I choose faithfulness . . .

Today I will keep my promises. My debtors will not regret their trust. My associates will not question my word. My wife will not question my love. And my children will never fear that their father will not come home.

I choose gentleness . . .

Nothing is won by force. I choose to be gentle. If I raise my voice may it be only in praise. If I clench my fist, may it be only in prayer. If I make a demand, may it be only of myself.

I choose self-control . . .

I am a spiritual being. After this body is dead, my spirit will soar. I refuse to let what will rot, rule the eternal. I choose self-control. I will be drunk only by joy. I will be impassioned only by my faith. I will be influenced only by God. I will be taught only by Christ. I choose self-control.

Love, joy, peace, patience, kindness, goodness, faithfulness, gentleness, and self-control. To these I commit my day. If I succeed, I will give thanks. If I fail, I will seek His grace. And then, when this day is done, I will place my head on my pillow and rest.

CHAPTER TWELVE

The Prophet

I wanted breakfast. I got a prophet.

I stopped at the grocery store on the way to the office this morning. Had to run an errand and decided while I was there to run another. I went over to the *deli* to order some breakfast. For a couple of quid you can get all the eggs and sausage you can handle. My waistline and the doctor keep me from doing this every day, but since I was in the store anyway and since I hadn't eaten . . .

A prophet had the same idea. Not a prophet *in* the Bible, but a prophet *with* a Bible. A thick, dog-eared blue-bound Bible. He was short and thin—a wispy fellow with cropped, unkempt hair, and a bushy, red beard.

By the time I got there, he was already ordering his food. *Meticulously* ordering his food. 'Do you serve a breakfast *taco* with no meat?'

Yes.

'Just potatoes and eggs?'

Yes.

'Is it salted?'

No.

'How many potatoes?'

The *deli* lady lifted the pan so he could see.

'And how many *tacos*?'

Maybe he wanted to be sure he got his money's worth. Maybe he observes a religious diet. Or maybe he was just picky. I couldn't tell. But I could see that he was polite, painfully polite.

He carried a rake. (A modern version of the winnowing fork perhaps?) His robe was blue, and under it was a shirt that looked like a converted towel.

While one worker was preparing the prophet's food, a second appeared. He thought the prophet hadn't been waited on and asked if he needed help.

'No, I've been helped. But since you asked, may I ask you if you are a believer in Jesus Christ? I am his prophet and I am sent to you.'

The worker didn't know how to respond. He looked at the *deli* lady, who looked over her shoulder and shrugged. He looked at me, then looked away. Then he looked back at the prophet and mumbled something like, 'Thanks for coming,' and asked me if I needed any help.

I did and told him what I wanted. And while I waited, out came the *tacos* for the prophet. He'd ordered a soft drink—with no ice. And water—in a paper cup. He was surprised at the colour of his soft drink.

'I thought it would be orange.'

'No, it's clear,' the lady responded.

I half-hoped he'd try a miracle—changing the water from clear to orange. He didn't; he simply interpreted the moment. 'In life it really doesn't matter what colour your drinks are, does it?' He smiled at the lady, smiled at the man, and then smiled at me.

We all smiled back.

Since he had a Bible in one hand and a rake in the other,

I wondered how he was going to carry the food. So I offered to help. He declined.

'Thank you in the name of Jesus for offering to help, but I can make it.'

He stacked the plate on the top of the soft-drink cup and somehow picked up the water with the rake-holding, Bible-toting hand. In the process he almost lost it all, so I offered to help again.

'No, but in the name of Jesus I bless you for offering to help me.'

'And,' he turned to the *deli* lady, 'I bless you in the name of Jesus Christ for your kind assistance.'

'And,' he caught the glance of the *deli* man, 'I bless you in the name of Jesus Christ.' He didn't say what for. A generic blessing, I assumed.

Having blessed us, he turned to leave. As far as I know, he made it to the table.

I watched the eyes of the cashier as she rang up my breakfast. Knowing absolutely nothing about her, I wondered what she was thinking. I wondered what her encounter with the prophet had done for her opinion of the One whom the prophet represented.

I wanted to say something, but didn't know what to say. I started to say, 'Me and the prophet there, we are on the same team; we just have two different approaches. Being a Christian doesn't really mean carrying a rake.'

But before I could think what to say, she'd turned to help someone else. So I turned to leave.

That's when I bumped into Lawrence. Lawrence is a friend from my church. Bumping into Lawrence is no small matter. He's an ex-pro football player. Everything about Lawrence is big, and everything about Lawrence is kind. A strong hug from Lawrence can last you a week.

And that's what he gave me . . . a good hug, a warm

handshake, and a genuine question about my well-being. Not much, just a couple of minutes of kind concern. Then he went his way and I went mine.

As I was leaving, I was struck by the contrast of the two encounters. Both the prophet and Lawrence are followers of Christ. Both are unashamed of their faith. Both love to carry a Bible. Both like to bless people. But that's where the similarities end.

One wears sandals and a robe, and the other wears tennis shoes and jeans.

One dresses like Jesus, but the other acts like Jesus.

One introduced himself as an ambassador for Christ; the other didn't have to.

One stirred my curiosity, but the other touched my heart.

And something told me that if Jesus were here, in person, in San Antonio, and I ran into Him in a grocery store, I wouldn't recognise Him by his rake, robe, and big Bible. But I would know Him for His good heart and kind words.

PART TWO

The Touch
of the Master

In his later years Beethoven would spend hours playing a broken harpsichord. The instrument was worthless. Keys were missing. Strings were stretched. It was out of tune, harsh on the ears.

Nonetheless the great pianist would play till tears came down his cheeks. To look at him, you'd think he was hearing the sublime. He was. For he was deaf. Beethoven was hearing the sound the instrument should make, not the one it did make.[1]

Ever feel like Beethoven's harpsichord? Out of tune? Inadequate? Your service ill-timed, insignificant?

Ever wonder what God does when the instrument is broken? What happens to the song when the strings are out of tune? How does the Master respond when the keys don't work?

Does He turn and leave? Does He demand a replacement? Does He junk the old? Or does He patiently tune until He hears the song He longs to hear?

If you've asked those questions (and who hasn't?), I've got some thoughts for you to read. I've assembled a curious covey of testimonies I thought you'd enjoy. In the following pages, you'll find:

— an explanation of why the Wizard of Oz is not in the Bible
— an account of a moody moon
— an early newspaper interview with Moses and Jehoshaphat

— *the message of a cricket and the common diet of prechewed food.*

Some chapters are funny. Some serious. Some fictional. Some factual. But all have an answer for those who feel like Beethoven's harpsichord. All work together to encourage the tired instrument. All hope to show you how the Master Musician fixes what we can't and hears music when we don't.

CHAPTER THIRTEEN

When Crickets
Make You Cranky

Forgive me if this chapter is disjointed. As I write, I am angry. I am angered by a cricket. He's loud. He's obnoxious. He's hidden. And he's in big trouble if I ever find him.

I arrived at my office early. Two hours before my alarm sounded, I was here. Sleeves rolled back and computer humming. *Beat the phones*, I thought. *Get a jump on the morning*, I planned. *Get a leg up on the day.*

But *Get your hands on that cricket* is what I keep mumbling.

Now, I have nothing against nature. The melody of a canary, I love. The pleasant hum of the wind in the leaves, I relish. But the predawn *raack-raack-raack* of a cricket bugs me.

So I get on my knees and follow the sound through the office. I peek under boxes. I pull books off the shelves. I get on my stomach and look under my desk. Humbling. I've been sabotaged by a one-inch insedt.

What is this insolent irritant that reduces a man to stalking insects?

Finally, I isolate the culprit.

Rats, he's behind a shelf. Out of my reach. Hidden in a haven of plywood. I can't get to him. All I can do is throw pens at the base of the shelf. So I do. *Pop. Pop. Pop.* One after another. A barrage of biros. He finally shuts up.

But the silence lasts only a minute.

So forgive me if my thoughts are fragmented, but I'm launching artillery every other paragraph. This is no way to work. This is no way to start the day. My floor is cluttered. My trousers are dusty. My train of thought is derailed. I mean, how can you write about anger with a stupid cricket in your office?

Oooops. Guess I'm in the right frame of mind after all . . .

Anger. This morning it's easy to define: the noise of the soul. *Anger.* The unseen irritant of the heart. *Anger.* The relentless invader of silence.

Just like the cricket, anger irritates.

Just like the cricket, anger isn't easily silenced.

Just like the cricket, anger has a way of increasing in volume until it's the only sound we hear. The louder it gets the more desperate we become.

When we are mistreated, our animalistic response is to go on the hunt. Instinctively, we double up our fists. Getting even is only natural. Which, incidentally, is precisely the problem. Revenge is natural, not spiritual. Getting even is the rule of the jungle. Giving grace is the rule of the kingdom.

Some of you are thinking, *Easy for you to say, Max, sitting there in your office with a cricket as your chief irritant. You ought to try living with my wife.* Or, *You ought to have to cope with my past.* Or, *You ought to raise my kids. You don't know how my 'ex' has mistreated me. You don't have any idea how hard my life has been.*

And you're right, I don't. But I have a very clear idea how miserable your future will be unless you deal with your anger.

X-ray the soul of the vengeful and behold the tumour of bitterness: black, menacing, malignant. Carcinoma of the spirit. Its fatal fibres creep around the edge of the heart and ravage it. Yesterday you can't alter, but your reaction to yesterday you can. The past you cannot change, but your response to your past you can.

Impossible, you say? Let me try to show you otherwise.

Imagine you are from a large family—a dozen or so kids. A family more blended than the Brady bunch. All the children are from the same dad, but they have four or five different mums.

Imagine also that your dad is a sneak and has been one for a long time. Everybody knows it. Everybody knows he cheated your uncle out of the estate. Everybody knows he ran like a coward to avoid getting caught.

Let's also imagine that your great-uncle tricked your dad into marrying your mother's sister. He got your dad drunk before the wedding and had his ugly daughter go to the altar instead of the pretty one your dad thought he was marrying.

That didn't slow down your father, though. He just married them both. The one he loved couldn't have kids, so he slept with her maid. In fact, he had a habit of sleeping with most of the kitchen help; as a result, most of your siblings resemble the cooks.

Finally the bride your dad wanted to marry in the first place gets pregnant . . . and you are born.

You're the favoured son . . . and your brothers know it.

You get a car. They don't. You get Armani; they get K-Mart. You get summer camp; they get summer jobs. You get educated; they get angry.

And they get even. They sell you to some foreign service project, put you on a plane for Egypt, and tell your dad you got shot by a sniper. You find yourself surrounded by people you don't know, learning a language you don't understand,

and living in a culture you've never seen.

Imaginary tale? No. It's the story of Joseph. A favoured son in a bizarre family, he had every reason to be angry.

He tried to make the best of it. He became the chief servant of the head of the Secret Service. His boss's wife tried to seduce him, and when he refused, she pouted and he ended up in prison. Pharaoh got wind of the fact that Joseph could interpret dreams and let him take a shot at some of Pharaoh's own.

When Joseph interpreted them he got promoted out of the prison into the palace as prime minister. The second highest position in all of Egypt. The only person Joseph bowed before was the king.

Meanwhile a famine hits and Jacob, Joseph's father, sends his sons to Egypt for a foreign loan. The brothers don't know it, but they are standing in front of the same brother they sold to the Gypsies some twenty-two years earlier.

They don't recognize Joseph, but Joseph recognizes them. A bit balder and paunchier, but they are the same brothers. Imagine Joseph's thoughts. The last time he saw these faces, he was looking up at them from the bottom of a pit. The last time he heard these voices, they were laughing at him. The last time they called his name, they called him every name in the book.

Now is his chance to get even. He has complete control. One snap of his fingers and these brothers are dead. Better yet, slap some manacles on their hands and feet and let them see what an Egyptian dungeon is like. Let them sleep in the mud. Let them mop floors. Let them learn Egyptian.

Revenge is within Joseph's power. And there is power in revenge. Intoxicating power.

Haven't we tasted it? Haven't we been tempted to get even?

As we escort the offender into the courtroom, we

announce, 'He hurt me!' The jurors shake their heads in disgust. 'He abandoned me!' we explain, and the chambers echo with our accusation. 'Guilty!' the judge snarls as he slams the gavel. 'Guilty!' the jury agrees. 'Guilty!' the audience proclaims. We delight in this moment of justice. We relish this pound of flesh. So we prolong the event. We tell the story again and again and again.

Now let's freeze-frame that scene. I have a question. Not for all of you, but for a few of you. Some of you are in the courtroom. The courtroom of complaint. Some of you are rehashing the same hurt every chance you get with anyone who will listen.

For you, I have this question: who made you God? I don't mean to be cocky, but why are you doing His work for Him?

'Vengeance is Mine,' God declared. 'I will repay' (Heb. 10:30 NKJV).

'Don't say, "I'll pay you back for the wrong you did." Wait for the LORD, and he will make things right' (Prov. 20:22).

Judgement is God's job. To assume otherwise is to assume God can't do it.

Revenge is irreverent. When we strike back we are saying, 'I know vengeance is yours, God, but I just didn't think you'd punish enough. I thought I'd better take this situation into my own hands. You have a tendency to be a little soft.'

Joseph understands that. Rather than get even, he reveals his identity and has his father and the rest of the family brought to Egypt. He grants them safety and provides them a place to live. They live in harmony for seventeen years.

But then Jacob dies and the moment of truth comes. The brothers have a hunch that with Jacob gone they'll be lucky to get out of Egypt with their heads on their shoulders. So they go to Joseph and plead for mercy.

'Your father gave this command before he died. . . . "Tell

Joseph to forgive you" (Gen. 50:16–17). (I have to smile at the thought of grown men talking like this. Don't they sound like kids, whining, 'Daddy said to be nice to us'?)

Joseph's response? 'When Joseph received the message, he cried' (Gen. 50:17). *'What more do I have to do?'* his tears implore. *'I've given you a home. I've provided for your families. Why do you still mistrust my grace?'*

Please read carefully the two statements he makes to his brothers. First he asks, 'Can I do what only God can do?' (v. 19).

May I restate the obvious? Revenge belongs to God! If vengeance is God's, then it is not ours. God has not asked us to settle the score or get even. Ever.

Why? The answer is found in the second part of Joseph's statement: 'You meant to hurt me, but God turned your evil into good to save the lives of many people, which is being done' (v. 20).

Forgiveness comes easier with a wide-angle lens. Joseph uses one to get the whole picture. He refuses to focus on the betrayal of his brothers without also seeing the loyalty of his God.

It always helps to see the big picture.

Some time ago I was in an airport lounge when I saw an acquaintance enter. He was a man I hadn't seen in a while but had thought about often. He'd been through a divorce, and I was close enough to it to know that he deserved some of the blame.

I noticed he was not alone. Beside him was a woman. *Why, that scoundrel! Just a few months out and here he has another lady?*

Any thought of greeting him disappeared as I passed judgement on his character. But then he saw me. He waved at me. He motioned me over. I was caught. I was trapped. I'd have to go and talk to the reprobate. So I did.

'Max, meet my aunt and her husband.'

I gulped. I hadn't noticed the man.

'We're on our way to a family reunion. I know they would really like to meet you.'

'We use your books in our home Bible study,' my friend's uncle spoke up. 'You've got some great insights.'

'If only you knew,' I said to myself. I had committed a common sin of the unforgiving. I had cast a vote without knowing the story.

To forgive someone is to admit our limitations. We've been given only one piece of life's jigsaw puzzle. Only God has the cover of the box.

To forgive someone is to display reverence. Forgiveness is not saying the one who hurt you was right. Forgiveness is stating that God is fair and He will do what is right.

After all, don't we have enough things to do without trying to do God's work too?

Guess what. I just noticed something. The cricket is quiet. I got so wrapped up in this chapter I forgot him. I haven't thrown a pen for an hour. Guess he fell asleep. Could be that's what He wanted to do all along, but I kept waking him up with my biros.

He ended up getting some rest. I ended up finishing this chapter. Remarkable what gets accomplished when we let go of our anger.

CHAPTER FOURTEEN

Seeing What Eyes Can't

I stand six steps from the bed's edge. My arms extended. Hands open. On the bed Sara—all four years of her—crouches, posed like a playful kitten. She's going to jump. But she's not ready. I'm too close.

'Back more, Daddy,' she stands and dares.

I dramatically comply, confessing admiration for her courage. After two giant steps I stop. 'More?' I ask.

'Yes!' Sara squeals, hopping on the bed.

With each step she laughs and claps and motions for more. When I'm on the other side of the canyon, when I'm beyond the reach of mortal man, when I am but a tiny figure on the horizon, she stops me. 'There, stop there.'

'Are you sure?'

'I'm sure,' she shouts. I extend my arms. Once again she crouches, then springs. Superman without a cape. Skydiver without a chute. Only her heart flies higher than her body. In that airborne instant her only hope is her father. If he proves weak, she'll fall. If he proves cruel, she'll crash. If he proves forgetful, she'll tumble to the hard floor.

But such fear she does not know, for her father she does.

She trusts him. Four years under the same roof have convinced her he is reliable. He is not superhuman, but he is strong. He is not holy, but he is good. He's not brilliant, but he doesn't have to be to remember to catch his child when she jumps.

And so she flies.

And so she soars.

And so he catches her and the two rejoice at the wedding of her trust and his faithfulness.

I stand a few feet from another bed. This time no one laughs. The room is solemn. A machine pumps air into a tired body. A monitor metronomes the beats of a weary heart. The woman on the bed is no child. She was, once. Decades back. She was. But not now.

Like Sara, she must trust. Only days out of the operating room, she's just been told she'll have to return. Her frail hand squeezes mine. Her eyes mist with fear.

Unlike Sara, she sees no father. But the Father sees her. *Trust Him,* I say to us both. Trust the voice that whispers your name. Trust the hands to catch.

I sit across the table from a good man. Good and afraid. His fear is honest. Stocks are down. Inflation is up. He has a payroll to meet and bills to pay. He hasn't squandered or gambled or played. He has worked hard and prayed often, but now he's afraid. Beneath the flannel suit lies a timid heart.

He stirs his coffee and stares at me with the eyes of Wile E. Coyote who just realised he's run beyond the edge of a cliff. He's about to fall and fall fast. He's Peter on the water, seeing the storm and not the face. He's Peter in the waves, hearing the wind and not the voice.

Trust, I urge. But the word thuds. He's unaccustomed to such strangeness. He's a man of reason. Even when the kite flies beyond the clouds he still holds the string. But now the string has slipped. And the sky is silent.

I stand a few feet from a mirror and see the face of a man who failed . . . who failed his Maker. Again. I promised I wouldn't, but I did. I was quiet when I should have been bold. I took a seat when I should have taken a stand.

If this were the first time, it would be different. But it isn't. How many times can one fall and expect to be caught?

Trust. Why is it easy to tell others and so hard to remind self? Can God deal with death? I told the woman so. Can God deal with debt? I ventured as much with the man. Can God hear yet one more confession from these lips?

The face in the mirror asks.

I sit a few feet from a man on death row. Jewish by birth. Tentmaker by trade. Apostle by calling. His days are marked. I'm curious about what bolsters this man as he nears his execution. So I ask some questions.

Do you have family, Paul? *I have none.*

What about your health? *My body is beaten and tired.*

What do you own? *I have my parchments. My pen. A cloak.*

And your reputation? *Well, it's not much. I'm a heretic to some, a maverick to others.*

Do you have friends? *I do, but even some of them have turned back.*

Any awards? *Not on earth.*

Then what do you have, Paul? No belongings. No family. Criticised by some. Mocked by others. What do you have, Paul? What do you have that matters?

I sit back quietly and watch. Paul rolls his hand into a fist. He looks at it. I look at it. What is he holding? What does he have?

He extends his hand so I can see. As I lean forward, he opens his fingers. I peer at his palm. It's empty.

I have my faith. It's all I have. But it's all I need. I have kept the faith.

Paul leans back against the wall of his cell and smiles. And I lean back against another and stare into the face of a man who has learned that there is more to life than meets the eye.

For that's what faith is. Faith is trusting what the eye can't see.

Eyes see the prowling lion. Faith sees Daniel's angel.

Eyes see storms. Faith sees Noah's rainbow.

Eyes see giants. Faith sees Canaan.

Your eyes see your faults. Your faith sees your Saviour.

Your eyes see your guilt. Your faith sees His blood.

Your eyes see your grave. Your faith sees a city whose builder and maker is God.

Your eyes look in the mirror and see a sinner, a failure, a promise-breaker. But by faith you look in the mirror and see a robed prodigal bearing the ring of grace on your finger and the kiss of your Father on your face.

But wait a minute, someone asks. How do I know this is true? Nice prose, but give me the facts. How do I know these aren't just fanciful hopes?

Part of the answer can be found in Sara's little leaps of

faith. Her older sister, Andrea, was in the room watching, and I asked Sara if she would jump to Andrea. Sara refused. I tried to convince her. She wouldn't budge. 'Why not?' I asked.

'I only jump to big arms.'

If we think the arms are weak, we won't jump.

For that reason, the Father flexed His muscles. 'God's power is very great for those who believe,' Paul taught. 'That power is the same as the great strength God used to raise Christ from the dead' (Eph. 1:19–20).

Next time you wonder if God can catch you, read that verse. The very arms that defeated death are the arms awaiting you.

Next time you wonder if God can forgive you, read that verse. The very hands that were nailed to the cross are open for you.

And the next time you wonder if you will survive the jump, think of Sara and me. If a flesh-and-bone-headed dad like me can catch his child, don't you think your eternal Father can catch you?

CHAPTER FIFTEEN

Overcoming Your Heritage

Stefan can tell you about family trees. He makes his living from them. He inherited a German forest that has been in his family for 400 years. The trees he harvests were planted 180 years ago by his great-grandfather. The trees he plants won't be ready for market until his great-grandchildren are born.

He's part of a chain.

'Every generation must make a choice,' he told me. 'They can either pillage or plant. They can rape the landscape and get rich, or they can care for the landscape, harvest only what is theirs, and leave an investment for their children.'[1]

Stefan harvests seeds sown by men he never knew.

Stefan sows seeds to be harvested by descendants he'll never see.

Dependent upon the past, responsible for the future: he's part of a chain.

Like us. Children of the past, are we. Parents of the future. Heirs. Benefactors. Recipients of the work done by those before. Born into a forest we didn't seed.

Which leads me to ask, how's your forest?

As you stand on the land bequeathed by your ancestors, how does it look? How do you feel?

Pride at legacy left? Perhaps. Some inherit nourished soil. Deeply rooted trees of conviction. Row after row of truth and heritage. Could be that you stand in the forest of your fathers with pride. If so, give thanks, for many don't.

Many aren't proud of their family trees. Poverty. Shame. Abuse. Such are the forests found by some of you. The land was pillaged. Harvest was taken, but no seed was sown.

Perhaps you were reared in a home of bigotry and so you are intolerant of minorities. Perhaps you were reared in a home of greed, hence your desires for possessions are insatiable.

Perhaps your childhood memories bring more hurt than inspiration. The voices of your past cursed you, belittled you, ignored you. At the time, you thought such treatment was typical. Now you see it isn't.

And now you find yourself trying to explain your past.

I came across a story of a man who must have had such thoughts. His heritage was tragic. His grandfather was a murderer and a mystic who sacrificed his own children in ritual abuse. His dad was a punk who ravaged houses of worship and made a mockery of believers. He was killed at the age of twenty-four . . . by his friends.

The men were typical of their era. They lived in a time when prostitutes purveyed their wares in houses of worship. Wizards treated disease with chants. People worshipped stars and followed horoscopes. More thought went into superstition and voodoo than into the education of the children.

It was a dark time in which to be born. What do you do when your grandfather followed black magic, your father was a scoundrel, and your nation is corrupt?

Follow suit? Some assumed he would. Branded him as a

delinquent before he was born, a chip off the old rotten block. You can almost hear the people moan as he passes, 'Gonna be just like his dad.'

But they were wrong. He wasn't. He reversed the trend. He defied the odds. He stood like a dam against the trends of his day and re-routed the future of his nation. His achievements were so remarkable, we still tell his story twenty-six hundred years later.

The story of King Josiah. The world has seen wiser kings; the world has seen wealthier kings; the world has seen more powerful kings. But history has never seen a more courageous king than young Josiah.

Born some six hundred years before Jesus, Josiah inherited a fragile throne and a tarnished crown. The temple was in disarray, the Law was lost, and the people worshipped whatever god they desired. But by the end of Josiah's thirty-one-year reign, the temple had been rebuilt, the idols destroyed, and the law of God was once again elevated to a place of prominence and power.

The forest had been reclaimed.

Josiah's grandfather, King Manasseh, was remembered as the king who filled 'Jerusalem from one end to the other with [the people's] blood' (2 Kings 21:16). His father, King Amon, died at the hands of his own officers. 'He did what God said was wrong,' reads his epitaph.

The citizens formed a posse and killed the assassins, and eight-year-old Josiah ascended the throne. Early in his reign Josiah made a brave choice. 'He lived as his ancestor David had lived, and he did not stop doing what was right' (2 Kings 22:2).

He flipped through his family scrapbook until he found an ancestor worthy of emulation. Josiah skipped his dad's life and bypassed his grandpa's. He leapfrogged back in time until he found David and resolved, 'I'm going to be like him.'

The principle? We can't choose our parents, but we can choose our mentors.

And since Josiah chose David (who had chosen God), things began to happen.

> The people tore down the altars for the Baal
> gods as Josiah directed.
>
> Josiah cut down the incense altars.
> Josiah . . . broke up the Asherah idols
> and . . . beat them into powder.
>
> He burned the bones of the priests.
>
> Josiah broke down the altars.
>
> He cut down all the incense altars in all of
> Israel. (2 Chr. 34:4–5, 7)

Not what you call a public relations tour. But, then again, Josiah was not out to make friends. He was out to make a statement: 'What my fathers taught, I don't teach. What they embraced, I reject.'

And he wasn't finished. Four years later, at the age of twenty-six, he turned his attention to the temple. It was in a shambles. The people had allowed it to fall into disrepair. But Josiah was determined. Something had happened that fuelled his passion to restore the temple. A baton had been passed. A torch had been received.

Early in his reign he'd resolved to serve the God of his ancestor David. Now he chose to serve the God of someone else. Note 2 Chronicles 34:8: 'In Josiah's eighteenth year as king, he made Judah and the Temple pure again. He sent

Shaphan . . . to repair the Temple of the LORD, *the God of Josiah*' (emphasis mine).

God was *his* God. David's faith was Josiah's faith. He had found the God of David and made Him his own. As the temple was being rebuilt, one of the workers happened upon a scroll. On the scroll were the words of God given to Moses nearly a thousand years earlier.

When Josiah heard the words, he was shocked. He wept that his people had drifted so far from God that His Word was not a part of their lives.

He sent word to a prophetess and asked her, 'What will become of our people?'

She told Josiah that since he had repented when he heard the words, his nation would be spared the anger of God (see 2 Chr. 34:27). Incredible. An entire generation received grace because of the integrity of one man.

Could it be that God placed him on earth for that reason?

Could it be that God has placed you on earth for the same?

Maybe your past isn't much to brag about. Maybe you've seen raw evil. And now you, like Josiah, have to make a choice. Do you rise above the past and make a difference? Or do you remain controlled by the past and make excuses?

Many choose the latter.

Many choose the convalescent homes of the heart. Healthy bodies. Sharp minds. But retired dreams. Back and forth they rock in the chair of regret, repeating the terms of surrender. Lean closely and you will hear them: 'If only.' The white flag of the heart.

'If only . . .'

'If only I'd been born somewhere else . . .'

'If only I'd been treated fairly . . .'
'If only I'd had kinder parents, more money,
greater opportunities . . .'

'If only I'd been potty-trained sooner, spanked
less, or taught to eat without slurping.'

Maybe you've used those words. Maybe you have every
right to use them. Perhaps you, like Josiah, were hearing the
ten count before you even got into the ring. For you to find
an ancestor worth imitating, you, like Josiah, have to flip way
back in your family album.

If such is the case, let me show you where to turn. Put
down the scrapbook and pick up your Bible. Go to John's
gospel and read Jesus' words: 'Human life comes from
human parents, but spiritual life comes from the Spirit'
(John 3:6).

Think about that. Spiritual life comes from the Spirit!
Your parents may have given you genes, but God gives you
grace. Your parents may be responsible for your body, but
God has taken charge of your soul. You may get your looks
from your mother, but you get eternity from your Father,
your heavenly Father.

By the way, He's not blind to your problems. In fact, God
is willing to give you what your family didn't.

Didn't have a good father? He'll be your Father.

Through God you are a son; and, if you are
a son, then you are certainly an heir (Gal. 4:7
PHILLIPS).

Didn't have a good role model? Try God.

> You are God's children whom he loves, so try to
> be like him (Eph. 5:1).

Never had a parent who wiped away your tears? Think again. God has noted each one.

> You have seen me tossing and turning through
> the night. You have collected all my tears in
> your bottle! You have recorded every one in
> your book (Ps. 56:8 TLB).

God has not left you adrift on a sea of heredity. Just like Josiah, you cannot control the way your forefathers responded to God. But you can control the way you respond to Him. The past does not have to be your prison. You have a voice in your destiny. You have a say in your life. You have a choice in the path you take.

Choose well and some day—generations from now—your grandchildren and great-grandchildren will thank God for the seeds you sowed.

CHAPTER SIXTEEN

The Sweet Song of the Second Fiddle

For thousands of years, the relationship had been perfect. As far back as anyone could remember, the moon had faithfully reflected the sun's rays into the dark night. It was the greatest duo in the universe. Other stars and planets marvelled at the reliability of the team. Generation after generation of earthlings were captivated by the reflection. The moon became the symbol of romance, high hopes, and even nursery rhymes.

'Shine on, harvest moon,' the people would sing. And he did. Well, in a way he did. You see, the moon didn't actually shine. He reflected. He took the light given to him by the sun and redirected it toward the earth. A simple task of receiving illumination and sharing it.

You would think such a combo would last for ever. It almost did. But one day, a nearby star planted a thought in the moon's core.

'It must be tough being a moon,' the star suggested.

'What do you mean? I love it! I've got an important job to do. When it gets dark, people look to me for help. And I look to the sun. He gives me what I need and I give the people what they need. People depend on me to light up their world. And I depend on the sun.'

'So, you and the sun must be pretty tight.'

'Tight? Why, we are like Huntley and Brinkley, Hope and Crosby, Benny and Day . . .'

'Or maybe Edgar Bergen and Charlie McCarthy?'

'Who?'

'You know, the man and the dummy.'

'Well, I don't know about the dummy part.'

'That's exactly what I mean. You are the dummy. You don't have any light of your own. You depend on the sun. You're the sidekick. You don't have any name for yourself.'

'Name for myself?'

'Yeah, you've been playing second fiddle for too long. You need to step out on your own.'

'What do you mean?'

'I mean stop reflecting and start generating. Do your own thing. Be your own boss. Get people to see you for who you really are.'

'Who am I?'

'Well, you are, uh, well, uh, well, that's what you need to find out. You need to find out who you are.'

The moon paused and thought for a moment. What the star said made sense. Though he had never considered it, the moon was suddenly aware of all the inequities of the relationship.

Why should he have to work the night shift all the time? And why should he be the one the astronauts stepped on first? And why should he always be accused of making waves? And why don't the dogs and wolves howl at the sun for a change? And why should it be such an outrage to 'moon' while 'sunning' is an accepted practice?

'You are right!' asserted the moon. 'It's high time we had a solar-lunar equity up here.'

'Now you're talking,' prodded the star. 'Go and discover the real moon!'

Such was the beginning of the break up. Rather than turning his attention toward the sun, the moon began turning his attention toward himself.

He set out on the course of self-enhancement. After all, his complexion was a disgrace, so full of craters and all. His wardrobe was sadly limited to three sizes; full-length, half-cast, and quarter-clad. And his colouring was an anaemic yellow.

So, girded with determination, he set out to reach for the moon.

He ordered glacier packs for his complexion. He changed his appearance to include new shapes such as triangular and square. And for colouring he opted for a punk-rock orange. 'No one is going to call me cheese-face any more.'

The new moon was slimmed down and shaped up. His surface was as smooth as a baby's bottom. Everything was fine for a while.

Initially, his new look left him basking in his own moonlight. Passing meteors would pause and visit. Distant stars would call and compliment. Fellow moons would invite him over to their orbits to watch 'As the World Turns.'

He had friends. He had fame. He didn't need the sun—until the trends changed. Suddenly 'punk' was out and 'prep' was in. The compliments stopped and the giggles began as the moon was slow to realise that he was out of style. Just as he finally caught on and had his orange changed to pinstripe, the style went to 'country'.

It was the painful poking of the rhinestones into his surface that caused him to finally ask himself, 'What's this all for anyway? You're on the cover of the magazine one day and forgotten the next. Living off the praise of others is an erratic diet.'

For the first time since he'd begun his campaign to find himself, the moon thought of the sun. He remembered the good ol' millenniums when praise was not a concern. What people thought of him was immaterial since he wasn't in the business of getting people to look at himself. Any praise that came his way was quickly passed on to the boss. The sun's plan was beginning to dawn on the moon. 'He may have been doing me a favour.'

He looked down upon the earth. The earthlings had been getting quite a show. They never knew what to expect: first punk, then preppie, now country. Oddsmakers in Las Vegas were making bets as to whether the next style would be chic or macho. Rather than be the light of their world he was the butt of their jokes.

Even the cow refused to jump over him.

But it was the cold that bothered him the most. Absence from the sunlight left him with a persistent chill. No warmth. No glow. His full-length overcoat didn't help. It couldn't help; the shiver was from the inside, an icy shiver from deep within his core that left him feeling cold and alone.

Which is exactly what he was.

One night as he looked down upon the people walking in the dark, he was struck by the futility of it all. He thought of the sun. *He gave me everything I needed. I served a purpose. I was warm. I was content. I was . . . I was what I was made to be.*

Suddenly, he felt the old familiar warmth. He turned and there was the sun. The sun had never moved. 'I'm glad you're back,' the sun said. 'Let's get back to work.'

'You bet!' agreed the moon.

The coat came off. The roundness returned, and a light

was seen in the dark sky. A light even fuller. A light even brighter.

And to this day whenever the sun shines and the moon reflects and the darkness is illuminated, the moon doesn't complain or get jealous. He does what he was intended to do all along.

The moon beams.

CHAPTER SEVENTEEN

Your Sack of Stones

You have one. A sack. A burlap sack. Probably aren't aware of it, may not have been told about it. Could be you don't remember it. But it was given to you. A sack. An itchy, scratchy burlap sack.

You needed the sack so you could carry the stones. Rocks, boulders, pebbles. All sizes. All shapes. All unwanted.

You didn't request them. You didn't seek them. But you were given them.

Don't remember?

Some were rocks of rejection. You were given one the time you didn't pass the trial. It wasn't for lack of effort. Heaven only knows how much you practised. You thought you were good enough for the team. But the coach didn't. The instructor didn't. You thought you were good enough, but they said you weren't.

They and how many others?

You don't have to live long before you get a collection of stones. Make a poor grade. Make a bad choice. Make a mess. Get called a few names. Get mocked. Get abused.

And the stones don't stop with adolescence. I sent a letter

this week to an unemployed man who's been rejected in more than fifty interviews.

And so the sack gets heavy. Heavy with stones. Stones of rejection. Stones we don't deserve.

Along with a few we do.

Look into the burlap sack and you see that not all the stones are from rejections. There is a second type of stone. The stone of regret.

> Regret for the time you lost your temper.
> Regret for the day you lost control.
> Regret for the moment you lost your pride.
> Regret for the years you lost your priorities.
> And even regret for the hour you lost your innocence.

One stone after another, one guilty stone after another.

With time the sack gets heavy. We get tired. How can you have dreams for the future when all your energy is required to shoulder the past?

No wonder some people look miserable. The sack slows the step. The sack chafes. Helps explain the irritation on so many faces, the sag in so many steps, the drag in so many shoulders, and most of all, the desperation in so many acts.

You're consumed with doing whatever it takes to get some rest.

So you take the sack to the office. You resolve to work so hard you'll forget about the sack. You arrive early and stay late. People are impressed. But when it's time to go home, there is the sack—waiting to be carried out.

You carry the stones into happy hour. With a name like that, it must bring relief. So you set the sack on the floor, sit on the stool, and drink a few. The music gets loud and your head gets light. But then it's time to go and you look down and there is the sack.

You drag it into therapy. You sit on the couch with the sack at your feet and spill all your stones on the floor and name them one by one. The therapist listens. She empathises. Some helpful counsel is given. But when the time is up, you're obliged to gather the rocks and take them with you.

You get so desperate you try a weekend rendezvous. A little excitement. A risky embrace. A night of stolen passion. And for a moment the load is lighter. But then the weekend passes. Sunday's sun sets and awaiting you on Monday's doorstep is—you got it—your sack of regrets and rejections.

Some even take the sack to church. Perhaps religion will help, we reason. But instead of removing a few stones, some well-meaning but misguided preacher may add to the load. God's messengers sometimes give more hurt than help. And you might leave the church with a few new rocks in your sack.

The result? A person slugging his way through life, weighed down by the past. I don't know if you've noticed, but it's hard to be thoughtful when you're carrying a burlap sack. It's hard to be affirming when you are affirmation-starved. It's hard to be forgiving when you feel guilty.

Paul had an interesting observation about the way we treat people. He said it about marriage, but the principle applies in any relationship. 'The man who loves his wife loves himself' (Eph. 5:28). There is a correlation between the way you feel about yourself and the way you feel about others. If you are at peace with yourself—if you like yourself—you will get along with others.

The converse is also true. If you don't like yourself, if you are ashamed, embarrassed, or angry, other people are going to know it. The tragic part of the burlap-sack story is we tend to throw our stones at those we love.

Unless the cycle is interrupted.

Which takes us to the question, 'How *does* a person get relief?'

Which, in turn, takes us to one of the kindest verses in the Bible, 'Come to me, all of you who are tired and have heavy loads, and I will give you rest. Accept my teachings and learn from me, because I am gentle and humble in spirit, and you will find rest for your lives. The teaching I ask you to accept is easy; the load I give you to carry is light' (Matt. 11:28–29).

You knew I was going to say that. I can see you holding this book and shaking your head. 'I've tried that. I've read the Bible, I've sat on the pew—but I've never received relief.'

If that is the case, could I ask a delicate but deliberate question? Could it be that you went to religion and didn't go to God? Could it be that you went to a church, but never saw Christ?

'Come to me,' the verse reads.

It's easy to go to the wrong place. I did yesterday. I was in Portland, Maine, catching a flight to Boston. Went to the desk, checked my bag, got my ticket, and went to the gate. I went past security, took my seat, and waited for the flight to be called. I waited and waited and waited—

Finally, I went up to the desk to ask the attendant and she looked at me and said, 'You're at the wrong gate.'

Now, what if I'd pouted and sighed, 'Well, there must not be a flight to Boston. Looks like I'm stuck.'

You would have said to me, 'You're not stuck. You're just at the wrong gate. Go down to the right gate and try again.'

It's not that you haven't tried—you've tried for years to deal with your past. Alcohol. Affairs. Workaholism. Religion.

Jesus says He is the solution for weariness of soul.

Go to Him. Be honest with Him. Admit you have soul secrets you've never dealt with. He already knows what they are. He's just waiting for you to ask Him to help. He's just waiting for you to give Him your sack.

Go ahead. You'll be glad you did. (Those near to you will be glad as well . . . it's hard to throw stones when you've left your sack at the cross.)

CHAPTER EIGHTEEN

Of Oz and God

You, me, and Dorothy of *The Wizard of Oz*—we have a lot in common.

We all know what it's like to find ourselves in a distant land surrounded by strange people.

Though our chosen path isn't paved with yellow bricks, we still hope it will lead us home.

The witches of the East want more than our ruby slippers.

And Dorothy is not the first person to find herself surrounded by brainless, heartless, and spineless people.

We can relate to Dorothy.

But when Dorothy gets to the Emerald City the comparison is uncanny. For what the Wizard said to her, some think God says to us.

You remember the plot. Each of the chief characters comes to the Wizard with a need. Dorothy seeks a way home. The scarecrow wants wisdom. The tin man desires a heart. The lion needs courage. The Wizard of Oz, they've heard, could grant all four. So they come. Trembling and reverent, they come. They shiver in his presence and gasp at his power. And with all the courage they can muster, they present their requests.

His response? He will help *after* they demonstrate their worthiness. He will help as soon as they overcome the source of evil. Bring me the witch's broom, he says, and I will help you.

So they do. They scale the castle walls and make wax of the witch, and in the process, they make some startling discoveries. They discover they can overcome evil. They discover that, with a little luck, a quick mind can handle the best the worst has to give. And they discover they can do it all without the wizard.

Which is good because when they get back to Oz the foursome learn that the wizard is a wimp. The curtain is pulled back and the almighty is revealed. The one they worshipped and feared is, alas, a balding, podgy professor who can stage a good light show but can do nothing to solve their problems.

He redeems himself, however, by what he shows this band of pilgrims. (This is the part that makes me think the Wizard may have done a pulpit circuit before he landed the wizard position.) He tells Dorothy and company that all the power they need is the power they already have. He explains that the power to handle their problems was with them all along. After all, didn't the scarecrow display wisdom, the tin man compassion, and the lion courage when they dealt with the witch? And Dorothy doesn't need the help of Oz almighty; all she needs is a good hot-air balloon.

The movie ends with Dorothy discovering that her worst nightmare was in reality just a bad dream. That her somewhere-over-the-rainbow home was right where she'd always been. And that it's nice to have friends in high places, but in the end, it's up to you to find your own way home.

The moral of *The Wizard of Oz?* Everything you may need, you've already got.

The power you need is really a power you already have.

Just look deep enough, long enough, and there's nothing you can't do.

Sound familiar? Sound patriotic? Sound . . . Christian?

For years it did to me. I'm an offspring of sturdy stock. A product of a rugged, blue-collar culture that honoured decency, loyalty, hard work, and loved Bible verses like, 'God helps those who help themselves.' (No, it's not in there.)

'God started it and now we must finish it' was our motto. He's done His part; now we do ours. It's a fifty-fifty proposition. A do-it-yourself curriculum that majors in our part and minors in God's part.

'Blessed are the busy,' this theology proclaims, 'for they are the true Christians.'

No need for the supernatural. No place for the extraordinary. No room for the transcendent. Prayer becomes a token. (The real strength is within you, not 'up there.') Communion becomes a ritual. (The true hero is you, not Him.) And the Holy Spirit? Well, the Holy Spirit becomes anything from a sweet disposition to a positive mental attitude.

It's a wind-the-world-up-and-walk-away view of God. And the philosophy works . . . as long as you work. Your faith is strong, as long as you are strong. Your position is secure, as long as you are secure. Your life is good, as long as you are good.

But, alas, therein lies the problem. As the Teacher said, 'No one is good' (Matt. 19:17 NKJV). Nor is anyone always strong; nor is anyone always secure.

Do-it-yourself Christianity is not much encouragement to the done-in and worn-out.

Self-sanctification holds little hope for the addict.

'Try a little harder' is little encouragement for the abused.

At some point we need more than good advice; we need help. Somewhere on this journey home we realise that a fifty-fifty proposition is too little. We need more—more than a podgy wizard who thanks us for coming but tells us the trip was unnecessary.

We need help. Help from the inside out. The kind of help Jesus promised. 'I will ask the Father, and he will give you another Helper to be with you for ever—the Spirit of truth. The world cannot accept him, because it does not see him or know him. But you know him, because he lives with you and will be *in* you' (John 14:16-17, emphasis mine).

Note the final words of the verse. And in doing so, note the dwelling place of God—'in you'.

Not near us. Not above us. Not around us. But in us. In the part of us we don't even know. In the heart no one else has seen. In the hidden recesses of our being dwells, not an angel, not a philosophy, not a genie, but God.

Imagine that.

When my daughter Jenna was six years old, I came upon her standing in front of a full-length mirror. She was looking down her throat. I asked her what she was doing and she answered, 'I'm looking to see if God is in my heart.'

I chuckled and turned and then overheard her ask Him, 'Are You in there?' When no answer came, she grew impatient and spoke on His behalf. With a voice deepened as much as a six-year-old can, she said, 'Yes.'

She's asking the right question. 'Are You in there?' Could it be what they say is true? It wasn't enough for You to appear in a bush or dwell in the temple? It wasn't enough for You to become human flesh and walk on the earth? It wasn't enough to leave Your word and the promise of Your return? You had to go further? You had to take up residence in us?

'Do you not know,' Paul penned, 'that your body is the temple of the Holy Spirit?' (1 Cor. 6:19 NKJV).

Perhaps you didn't. Perhaps you didn't know God would

go that far to make sure you got home. If not, thanks for letting me remind you.

The wizard says 'look inside yourself and find self.' God says 'look inside yourself and find God.' The first will get you to Kansas.

The latter will get you to heaven.

Take your pick.

CHAPTER NINETEEN

An Inside Job

*S*pray paint won't fix rust.

A Band-Aid won't remove a tumour.

Wax on the bonnet won't cure the cough of a car-engine.

If the problem is inside, you have to go inside.

I learned that this morning. I rolled out of bed early . . . really early. So early that Denalyn tried to convince me not to go to the office. 'It's the middle of the night,' she mumbled. 'What if a burglar tries to break in?'

But I'd been on holiday for a couple of weeks, and I was rested. My energy level was as high as the stack of things to do on my desk, so I drove to the church.

I must confess that the empty streets did look a bit scary. And there was that attempted break-in at the office a few weeks back. So I decided to be careful. I entered the office complex, disarmed the alarm, and then re-armed it so it would sound if anyone tried to enter.

Brilliant, I thought.

I had been at my desk for only a few seconds when the sirens screamed. *Somebody is trying to get in!* I raced down the hall, turned off the alarm, ran back to my office, and phoned the police. After I hung up, it occurred to me that the thieves could get in before the police arrived. I dashed back down the hall and re-armed the system.

'They won't get me,' I mumbled defiantly as I punched in the code.

As I turned to go back to the office, the sirens blared again. I disarmed the alarm and reset it. I could just picture those frustrated burglars racing back into the shadows every time they set off the alarm.

I walked to a window to look for the police. When I did, the alarm sounded a third time. *Hope the police get here soon,* I thought as I again disarmed and reset the alarm.

I was walking back to my office when—that's right—the alarm sounded again. I disarmed it and paused. *Wait a minute; this alarm system must be fouled up.*

I went back to my office to call the alarm company. *Just my luck,* I thought as I dialled, *of all the nights for the system to malfunction.*

'Our alarm system keeps going off,' I told the fellow who answered. 'We've either got some determined thieves or a malfunction.'

Miffed, I drummed my fingers on my desk as he called up our account.

'There could be one other option,' he volunteered.

'What else?'

'Did you know that your building is equipped with a motion detector?'

Oh boy.

About that time I saw the lights from the police car. I walked outside. 'Uh, I think the problem is on the inside, not the outside,' I told them.

They were nice enough not to ask for details, and I was embarrassed enough not to volunteer any. But I did learn a lesson: *you can't fix an inside problem by going outside.*

I spent an hour hiding from thieves who weren't there, faulting a system that hadn't failed, and calling for help I didn't need. I thought the problem was out there. All along it was in here.

Am I the only one to ever do that? Am I the only one to blame an inside problem on an outside source?

Alarms sound in your world as well. Maybe not with bells and horns, but with problems and pain. Their purpose is to signal impending danger. A fit of anger is a red flare. Uncontrolled debt is a flashing light. A guilty conscience is a warning sign indicating trouble within. Icy relationships are posted notices announcing anything from neglect to abuse.

You have alarms in your life. When they go off, how do you respond? Be honest, now. Hasn't there been a time or two when you went outside for a solution when you should have gone inward?

Ever blamed your plight on Washington? (If they'd lower the tax rates, my business would work.) Inculpated your family for your failure? (Mum always liked my sister more.) Called God to account for your problems? (If He is God, why doesn't He heal my marriage?) Faulted the church for your frail faith? (Those people are a bunch of hypocrites.)

Reminds me of the golfer about to hit his first shot on the first hole. He swung and missed the ball. Swung again and whiffed again. Tried a third time and still hit nothing but air. In frustration he looked at his buddies and judged, 'Man, this is a tough course.'

Now, he may have been right. The course may have been tough. But that wasn't the problem. You may be right, as well. Your circumstances may be challenging, but blaming them is not the solution. Nor is neglecting them. Heaven knows you don't silence life's alarms by pretending they aren't screaming. But heaven also knows it's wise to look in the mirror before you peek out the window.

Consider the prayer of David: 'Create *in* me a new heart, O God, and renew a steadfast spirit *within* me' (Ps. 51:10 NIV).

Read the admonition of Paul: 'Fix your attention on God. You'll be changed from the *inside out*' (Rom. 12:2 THE MESSAGE).

But most of all, listen to the explanation of Jesus: 'I tell you the truth, unless one is born again, he cannot be in God's kingdom' (John 3:3).

Real change is an inside job. You might alter things a day or two with money and systems, but the heart of the matter is and always will be, the matter of the heart.

Allow me to get specific. Our problem is sin. Not finances. Not budgets. Not overcrowded prisons or drug dealers. Our problem is sin. We are in rebellion against our Creator. We are separated from our Father. We are cut off from the source of life. A new president or policy won't fix that. It can only be solved by God.

That's why the Bible uses drastic terms like *conversion, repentance,* and *lost* and *found.* Society may renovate, but only God re-creates.

Here is a practical exercise to put this truth into practice. The next time alarms go off in your world, ask yourself three questions.

1. Is there any unconfessed sin in my life?

'There was a time when I wouldn't admit what a sinner I was. But my dishonesty made me miserable and filled my days with frustration. . . . My strength evaporated like water on a sunny day until I finally admitted all my sins to you and stopped trying to hide them' (Ps. 32:3–5 TLB).

(Confession is telling God you did the thing He saw you

do. He doesn't need to hear it as much as you need to say it. Whether it's too small to be mentioned or too big to be forgiven isn't yours to decide. Your task is to be honest.)

2. Are there any unresolved conflicts in my world?

'If you enter a place of worship and, about to make an offering, suddenly remember a grudge that a friend has against you, abandon your offering, leave immediately, go to this friend and make things right. Then and only then, come back and work things out with God' (Matt. 5:23–24 THE MESSAGE).

(As far as I know, this is the only time God tells you to slip out of church early. Apparently, He'd rather have you give your olive branch than your tithe. If you are worshipping and remember that your mum is annoyed with you for forgetting her birthday, then get off the pew and find a phone. Maybe she'll forgive you; maybe she won't. But at least you can return to your pew with a clean conscience.)

3. Are there any unsurrendered worries in my heart?

'Give all your worries to him, because he cares about you' (1 Pet. 5:7).

(The German word for *worry* means 'to strangle.' The Greek word means 'to divide the mind'. Both are accurate. Worry is a noose on the neck and a distraction of the mind, neither of which is befitting for joy.)

Alarms serve a purpose. They signal a problem. Sometimes the problem is out there. More often it's in here. So before you peek outside, take a good look inside.

CHAPTER TWENTY

Late-Night Good News

$\mathcal{L}$ate-night news is a poor sedative.

Last night it was for me. All I wanted was the pollen count and the basketball scores. But to get them, I had to endure the usual monologue of global misery. And last night the world seemed worse than usual.

Watching the news doesn't usually disturb me so. I'm not a gloom-and-doom sort of fellow. I feel I'm as good as the next guy in taking human tragedy with a spoon of faith. But last night . . . well, the world seemed dark.

Perhaps it was the two youngsters shot in a drive-by shooting—one was six, the other ten.

Perhaps it was the reassuring announcement that twenty-six thousand highway bridges in America are near collapse.

Our surgeon general, who is opposed to tobacco, wants to legalise drugs.

A billionaire rock star is accused of molesting children. One senator is accused of seducing associates, another of tampering with election procedures.

A rising political figure in Russia has earned the nickname of Hitler.

Pistol-packing drivers give rise to a new bumper sticker: 'Keep honking. I'm reloading.'

The national debt is deeper. Our taxes are higher, the pollen count is up, and the Dallas Mavericks lost their fifteenth game in a row.

'And that's the world tonight!' the well-dressed man announces. I wonder why he's smiling.

On the way to bed, I step into the rooms of my three sleeping daughters. At the bedside of each I pause and ponder the plight of their future. 'What in the world awaits you?' I whisper as I brush back hair and straighten blankets.

Their greatest concerns today are maths tests, presents, and birthday parties. Would that their world would always be so innocent. It won't. Forests shadow every trail, and cliffs edge every turn. Every life has its share of fear. My children are no exception.

Nor are yours. And as appealing as a desert island or a monastery might be, seclusion is simply not the answer for facing a scary tomorrow.

Then what is? Does someone have a hand on the throttle of this train, or has the engineer bailed out just as we come in sight of dead-man's curve?

I may have found part of the answer in, of all places, the first chapter of the New Testament. I've often thought it strange that Matthew would begin his book with a genealogy. Certainly not good journalism. A list of who-sired-who wouldn't get past most editors.

But then again, Matthew wasn't a journalist, and the Holy Spirit wasn't trying to get our attention. He was making a point. God had promised He would give a Messiah through the bloodline of Abraham (Gen. 12:3), and He did.

'Having doubts about the future?' Matthew asks. 'Just take a look at the past.' And with that he opens the cedar chest of Jesus' lineage and begins pulling out the dirty laundry.

Believe me, you and I would have kept some of these stories in the cupboard. Jesus' lineage is anything but a roll call at the Institute for Halos and Harps. Reads more like the Sunday morning occupancy at the county jail.

It begins with Abraham, the father of the nation, who more than once lied like Pinocchio just to save his neck (Gen. 12:10–20).

Abraham's grandson Jacob was slicker than a Las Vegas card shark. He cheated his brother, lied to his father, got swindled, and then swindled his uncle (Genesis 27, 29).

Jacob's son Judah was so blinded by testosterone that he engaged the services of a streetwalker, not knowing she was his daughter-in-law! When he learned her identity, he threatened to have her burned to death for solicitation (Genesis 38).

Special mention is made of Solomon's mother, Bathsheba (who bathed in questionable places), and Solomon's father, David, who watched the bath of Bathsheba (2 Sam. 11:2–3).

Rahab was a harlot (Josh. 2:1). Ruth was a foreigner (Ruth 1:4).

Manasseh made the list, even though he forced his children to walk through fire (2 Kings 21:6). His son Amon is on the list, even though he rejected God (2 Kings 21:22).

Seems that almost half the kings were crooks, half embezzlers, and all but a handful worshipped an idol or two for good measure.

And so reads the list of Jesus' not-so-great grandparents. Seems like the only common bond between this lot was a promise. A promise from heaven that God would use them to send His Son.

Why did God use these people? Didn't have to. Could

have just laid the Saviour on a doorstep. Would have been simpler that way. And why does God tell us their stories? Why does God give us an entire testament of blunders and stumbles of His people?

Simple. He knew what you and I watched on the news last night. He knew you would fret. He knew I would worry. And He wants us to know that when the world goes wild, He stays calm.

Want proof? Read the last name on the list. In spite of all the crooked halos and tasteless gambols of His people, the last name on the list is the first one promised—Jesus.

'Joseph was the husband of Mary, and Mary was the mother of Jesus. Jesus is called the Christ' (Matt. 1:16).

Period. No more names are listed. No more are needed. As if God is announcing to a doubting world, 'See, I did it. Just like I said I would. The plan succeeded.'

The famine couldn't starve it.

Four hundred years of Egyptian slavery couldn't? oppress it.

Wilderness wanderings couldn't lose it.

Babylonian captivity couldn't stop it.

Clay-footed pilgrims couldn't spoil it.

The promise of the Messiah threads its way through forty-two generations of rough-cut stones, forming a necklace fit for the King who came. Just as promised.

And the promise remains.

> Those people who keep their faith until the end will be saved (Matt. 24:13), Joseph's child assures.

> In this world you will have trouble, but be brave! I have defeated the world. (John 16:33)

The engineer has not abandoned the train. Nuclear war is no threat to God. Yo-yo economies don't intimidate the heavens. Immoral leaders have never derailed the plan.

God keeps His promise.

See for yourself. In the manger. He's there.

See for yourself. In the tomb. He's gone.

CHAPTER TWENTY-ONE

Healthy Habits

I like the story of the little boy who fell out of bed. When his Mum asked him what happened, he answered, 'I don't know. I guess I stayed too close to where I got in.'

Easy to do the same with our faith. It's tempting just to stay where we got in and never move.

Pick a time in the not-too-distant past. A year or two ago. Now ask yourself a few questions. How does your prayer life today compare with then? How about your giving? Have both the amount and the joy increased? What about your church loyalty? Can you tell you've grown? And Bible study? Are you learning to learn?

> We will in all things *grow up* into him who is the Head, that is, Christ (Eph. 4:15 NIV, emphasis mine).

> Let us leave the elementary teachings about Christ and go on to *maturity* (Heb. 6:1 NIV, emphasis mine).

Like newborn babies, crave pure spiritual milk,
so that by it you may *grow up* in your salvation
(1 Pet. 2:2 NIV, emphasis mine).

But *grow* in the grace and knowledge of our
Lord and Saviour Jesus Christ (2 Pet. 3:18 NIV,
emphasis mine).

Growth is the goal of the Christian. Maturity is mandatory. If a child ceased to develop, the parent would
be concerned, right? Doctors would be called. Tests would be
run. When a child stops growing, something is wrong.

When a Christian stops growing, help is needed. If you are
the same Christian you were a few months ago, be careful. You
might be wise to get a check up. Not on your body, but on
your heart. Not a medical, but a spiritual.

May I suggest one?

At the risk of sounding like a preacher—which is what I
am—may I make a suggestion? Why don't you check your
habits? Though there are many bad habits, there are also
many good ones. In fact, I can find four in the Bible. Make
these four habits regular activities and see what happens.

First, the habit of prayer: 'Base your happiness on your
hope in Christ. When trials come endure them patiently;
steadfastly maintain the *habit* of prayer' (Rom. 12:12
PHILLIPS, emphasis mine).

Do you want to know how to deepen your prayer life?
Pray. Don't prepare to pray. Just pray. Don't read about
prayer. Just pray. Don't attend a lecture on prayer or engage
in discussion about prayer. Just pray.

Posture, tone, and place are personal matters. Select the
form that works for you. But don't think about it too much.

Don't be so concerned about wrapping the gift that you never give it. Better to pray awkwardly than not at all.

And if you feel you should only pray when inspired, that's OK. Just see to it that you are inspired every day.

Second, the habit of study: 'The man who looks into the perfect law . . . and makes a *habit* of so doing, is not the man who hears and forgets. He puts that law into practice and he wins true happiness' (James 1:25 PHILLIPS, emphasis mine).

Imagine you are selecting your food from a cafeteria line. You pick your salad, you choose your *entrée*, but when you get to the vegetables, you see a pan of something that turns your stomach.

'Yuck! What's that?' you ask, pointing.

'Oh, you don't want to know,' replies a slightly embarrassed server.

'Yes, I do.'

'Well, if you must. It's a pan of pre-chewed food.'

'What?'

'Pre-chewed food. Some people prefer to swallow what others have chewed.'

Repulsive? You bet. But widespread. More so than you might imagine. Not with cafeteria food, but with God's Word.

Such Christians mean well. They listen well. But they discern little. They are content to swallow whatever they are told. No wonder they've stopped growing.

Third, the habit of giving: 'On *every Lord's Day* each of you should put aside something from what you have earned during the week, and use it for this offering. The amount depends on how much the Lord has helped you earn' (1 Cor. 16:2 TLB, emphasis mine).

You don't give for God's sake. You give for your sake. 'The purpose of tithing is to teach you to always put God first in your lives' (Deut. 14:23 TLB).

How does tithing teach you? Consider the simple act of writing a cheque for the offering. First you enter the date. Already you are reminded that you are a time-bound creature and every possession you have will rust or burn. Best to give it while you can.

Then you enter the name of the one to whom you are giving the money. If the bank would cash it, you'd write *God*. But they won't, so you write the name of the church or group that has earned your trust.

Next comes the amount. Ahhh, the moment of truth. You're more than a person with a cheque book. You're David, placing a stone in the sling. You're Peter, one foot on the boat, one foot on the lake. You're a little boy in a big crowd. A picnic lunch is all the Teacher needs, but it's all you have.

What will you do?

Sling the stone?

Take the step?

Give the meal?

Careful now, don't move too quickly. You aren't just entering an amount . . . you are making a confession. A confession that God owns it all anyway.

And then the line in the lower left-hand corner on which you write what the cheque is for. Hard to know what to put. It's for light bills and literature. A little bit of outreach. A little bit of salary.

Better yet, it's partial payment for what the church has done to help you raise your family . . . keep your own priorities sorted out . . . tune you in to His ever-nearness.

Or, perhaps, best yet, it's for you. For though the gift is to God, the benefit is for you. It's a moment for you to clip yet another strand from the rope of earth so that when He returns you won't be tied up.

And last of all, the habit of fellowship: 'Let us not give up the *habit* of meeting together, as some are doing. Instead let us encourage one another' (Heb. 10:25 TEV, emphasis mine).

I'm writing this chapter on a Saturday morning in Boston. I came here to speak at a conference. After I did my part last night, I did something very spiritual: I went to a Boston Celtics basketball game. I couldn't resist. Boston Gardens is a stadium I'd wanted to see since I was a kid. Besides, Boston was playing my favourite team, the San Antonio Spurs.

As I took my seat, it occurred to me that I might be the only Spurs fan in the crowd. I'd be wise to be quiet. But that was hard to do. I contained myself for a few moments, but that's all. By the end of the first quarter I was letting out solo war whoops every time the Spurs scored.

People were beginning to turn and look. Risky stuff, this voice-in-the-wilderness routine.

That's when I noticed I had a friend across the aisle. He, too, applauded the Spurs. When I clapped, he clapped. I had a partner. We buoyed each other. I felt better.

At the end of the quarter I gave him the thumbs-up. He gave it back. He was only a teenager. No matter. We were united by the higher bond of fellowship.

That's one reason for the church. All week you cheer for the visiting team. You applaud the success of the One the world opposes. You stand when everyone sits and sit when everyone stands.

At some point you need support. You need to be with folks who cheer when you do. You need what the Bible calls *fellowship*. And you need it every week. After all, you can only go so long before you think about joining the crowd.

∞

    There they are. Four habits worth having. Isn't it good to know that some habits are good for you? Make them a part of your day and grow. Don't make the mistake of the little boy. Don't stay too close to where you got in. It's risky resting on the edge.

CHAPTER TWENTY-TWO

DFW and the Holy Spirit

The Dallas-Fort Worth International Airport can be fatal. It doesn't have concourses—it has catacombs. Lobbies empty into labyrinths. People have been known to go into that airport and never come out.

Frequent flyers are easily distinguished from the first-timers. They're the ones with backpacks, compasses, canteens, and walking sticks. The novices bear the haggard faces, hollow eyes, and distant stares.

One of my first times through the maze was on a trip home from Brazil. I'd been flying all night and was a bit anxious about making my connections. I stopped one family of five and asked where I could get information. The parents looked at me as if they were the only survivors of a nuclear disaster.

The mother held up three fingers and gasped, 'Three days we have been here, and we still haven't found our connecting flight.'

I gulped. The dad asked if I could spare five dollars for a pizza for his kids. I gave him the money, and he pointed me toward a map of the airport.

The map was easy to find; it covered an entire wall. When I found the 'You are here' sign, I began looking for the gate of my next flight. When I saw where I was as opposed to where I needed to be, I gulped again. The Appalachian Trail would have been easier.

But I had no choice. I took a deep breath, gripped my satchel in one hand and my garment bag in the other, and set my face toward gate 6,690.

The floor was littered with travel bags discarded by weary pilgrims. People were falling to my right and to my left. Airport migrants hovered around water fountains as they would an oasis. Travellers fought over luggage trolleys.

I began to doubt if I would make it. Three hours into my trip, my knees began to ache. Five hours into the journey my hands grew raw from my bags. At the seven-hour mark, I began to hallucinate, seeing my gate number appear on the horizon only to have it grow wavy and disappear as I came near.

By the tenth hour, I had discarded my garment bag and was carrying only my briefcase. I was about to chuck it when I heard the cheering.

It was coming from the corridor up ahead. People were shouting. Some were running.

What was it? What could stir the hope of this trail of despairing pilgrims? What sight could strengthen these exhausted legs? A hotel? An empty restaurant? An available flight?

No, it was something far better. As I turned the corner, I saw it. My face lit like the night sky on the Fourth of July. I took the bandana off my head and wiped my brow. I straightened my back. I hastened my pace. My heart soared. Now, I knew, I would make it.

For there, in the distance, covered with lights and plated in gold, was a people-mover.

A people-mover. The Yellow Brick Road of the airport. It's the bridge across the Jordan. It's the downhill stretch for the marathon runner, the final lap for the athlete, the pay cheque for the worker, the final draft for the writer.

The people-mover, a path of progressive rest. Once on the people-mover, you don't have to move, but you still move! And while you are catching your breath, it's carrying your body.

But it's also a path of multiplied movement. For when you begin walking on it, every step is doubled. The propelling trail makes two steps out of your one. What would have taken an hour takes minutes.

And what a difference the people-mover makes on your attitude. You actually whistle as you walk. The fatigue is forgotten. The galumph is gone. Troops of travellers wave to each other.

And most important, you dare to believe again that you will reach your destination.

Now, maybe I overstated my point about the airport.

But I could never overstate the power of discovering strength for the journey. What I discovered about DFW you've discovered about life. No matter how you travel, the trip can get tiring. Wouldn't it be great to discover a people-mover for your heart?

Paul did. Well, he didn't call it as such. But then, he never went to DFW. He did say, however, that there is a power that works in you as you work. 'We proclaim him, admonishing and teaching everyone with all wisdom, so that we may present everyone perfect in Christ. To this end I labour, struggling with all his energy, which so powerfully works in me' (Col. 1:28 NIV).

Look at Paul's aim, *to present everyone perfect in Christ.* Paul dreamed of the day each person would be safe in Christ. What was his method? *Counselling and teaching.* Paul's tools?

Verbs. Nouns. Sentences. Lessons. The same equipment you and I have. Not much has changed, has it?

Was it easier then than now? Don't think so. Paul called it work. *To this end I labour,* he wrote. Labour means work. Work means homes visited, people taught, classes prepared.

How did he do it? What was his source of strength? He worked with *all the energy He so powerfully works in me.*

As Paul worked, so did God. As Paul laboured, so did the Father. And as you work, so does the Father. Every step multiplied. Divine dividends paid. Like the people-mover, God energises our efforts. And like the people-mover, God moves us forward. And even when we are too tired to walk, He ensures we are moving ahead.

So the next time you need to rest, go ahead. He'll keep you headed in the right direction. And the next time you make progress—thank Him. He's the one providing the power.

And the next time you want to give up? Don't. Please don't. Turn the next corner. You may be surprised at what you find.

Besides, you've got a flight home you don't want to miss.

CHAPTER TWENTY-THREE

The God Who Fights for You

Here is a big question. What is God doing when you are in a bind? When the lifeboat springs a leak? When the rip cord snaps? When the last penny is gone before the last bill is paid? When the last hope left on the last train? What is God doing?

I know what we are doing. Nibbling on nails like corn on the cob. Pacing floors. Taking pills. I know what we do.

But what does God do? Big question. Real big. If God is sleeping, I'm duck soup. If He is laughing, I'm lost. If He is crossing His arms and shaking His head, then saw off the limb, Honey, it's time to crash.

What *is* God doing?

Well, I decided to research that question. Being the astute researcher that I am, I discovered some ancient writings that may answer this question. Few people are aware—in fact, no one is aware—that newspaper journalists roamed the lands of the Old Testament era.

Yes, it is true that in the days of Noah, Abraham, and Moses, reporters were fast on the scene recording the drama of their days. And now, for the first time, their articles are to be shared.

How did I come upon them? one might ask.

Well, I discovered them pressed between the pages of an in-flight magazine on a red-eye flight out of Sheboygan, Wisconsin. I can only surmise that a courageous archaeologist had hidden them to protect himself from imminent danger of evil spies. We'll never know if he survived. But we do know what he discovered—ancient newspaper interviews with Moses and Jehoshaphat.

So with a salute to his courage and a hunger for the truth, I proudly share with you heretofore undiscovered conversations with two men who will answer the question: what does God do when we are in a bind?

The first interview is between the *Holy Land Press* (HLP) and Moses.

HLP: Tell us about your conflict with the Egyptians.

MOSES: Oh, the Egyptians—big people. Strong fighters. Mean as snakes.

HLP: But you got away.

MOSES: Not before they got washed away.

HLP: You're talking about the Red Sea conflict.

MOSES: You're right. That was scary.

HLP: Tell us what happened.

MOSES: Well, the Red Sea was on one side and the Egyptians were on the other.

HLP: So you attacked?

MOSES: Are you kidding? With a half-a-million rock stackers? No, my people were too afraid. They wanted to go back to Egypt.

HLP: So you told everyone to retreat?

MOSES: Where? Into the water? We didn't have a boat. We didn't have anywhere to go.

HLP: What did your leaders recommend?

MOSES: I didn't ask them. There wasn't time.

HLP: Then what did you do?

MOSES: I told the people to stand still.

HLP: You mean, with the enemy coming, you told them not to move?

MOSES: Yep. I told the people, 'Stand still and you will see the Lord save you.'

HLP: Why would you want the people to stand still?

MOSES: To get out of God's way. If you don't know what to do, it's best just to sit tight till He does his thing.

HLP: That's odd strategy, don't you think?

MOSES: It is if you are big enough for the battle. But when the battle is bigger than you are and you want God to take over, it's all you can do.

HLP: Can we talk about something else?

MOSES: It's your paper.

HLP: Soon after your escape . . .

MOSES: Our deliverance.

HLP: What's the difference?

MOSES: There is a big difference. When you escape, *you* do it. When you are delivered, someone else does it and you just follow.

HLP: OK, soon after your deliverance, you battled with the Ammo . . . Amala . . . let's see, I have it here . . .

MOSES: The Amalekites.

HLP: Yeah, the Amalekites.

MOSES: Big people. Strong fighters. Mean as snakes.

HLP: But you won.

MOSES: God won.

HLP: OK—God won—but you did the work. You fought the battle. You were on the field.

MOSES: Wrong.

HLP: What? You weren't in the battle?

MOSES: Not that one. While the army was fighting, I took my friends Aaron and Hur to the top of a hill and we did our fighting up there.

HLP: With each other?

MOSES: With the darkness.

HLP: With swords?

MOSES: No, in prayer. I just lifted my hands to God, like I did at the Red Sea, only this time I forgot my rod. When I lifted my hands, we would win, but when I would lower my arms we would lose. So I got my friends to hold up my arms until the Amalekites were history and we won.

HLP: Hold on a second. You think that standing on a hill with your hands in the air made a difference?

MOSES: You don't see any Amalekites around, do you?

HLP: Don't you think it strange that the general of the army stays on the mountain while the soldiers fight in the valley?

MOSES: If the battle had been in the valley I would have gone, but that's not where the battle was being fought.

HLP: Odd, this strategy of yours.

MOSES: You mean if your father was bigger than the fellow beating you up, you wouldn't call his name?

HLP: What?

MOSES: If some guy has you on the ground pounding on you and your father is within earshot and tells you to call him anytime you need help, what would you do?

HLP: I'd call my father.

MOSES: That's all I do. When the battle is too great, I ask God to take over. I get the Father to fight for me.

HLP: And He comes?

MOSES: Seen any Jews building pyramids lately?

HLP: Let me see if I've got this straight. Once you defeat the enemy by standing still and another time you win the battle by holding up your hands. Where did you pick all this up?

MOSES: Well, if I told you, you wouldn't believe me.

HLP: Try me.

MOSES: Well, you see, there was this bush on fire and it spoke to me . . .

HLP: Maybe you're right. We'll save that one for another day.

∞

The second interview moves us ahead in history a couple of centuries. Here is King Jehoshaphat (KJ) in a postwar interview with the *Jerusalem Chronicle* (JC) on the battlefield of Ziz.

JC: Congratulations, King.

KJ: For what?

JC: You just defeated three armies at once. You defeated the Moabites, Ammonites, and Meunites.

KJ: Oh, I didn't do that.

JC: Don't be so modest. Tell us what you think of these armies.

KJ: Big people. Strong fighters. Mean as snakes.

JC: How did you feel when you heard they were coming?

KJ: I was scared.

JC: But you handled it pretty calmly. That strategy session with your generals must have paid off.

KJ: We didn't have one.

JC: You didn't have a meeting, or you didn't have a strategy?

KJ: Neither.

JC: What did you do?

KJ: I asked God what to do.

JC: What did He say?

KJ: Nothing at first, so I got some people to talk to Him with me.

JC: Your cabinet had a prayer session?

KJ: No, my nation went on a fast.

JC: The whole nation?

KJ: Everyone but you, apparently.

JC: Uh, well, what did you tell God?

KJ: Well, we told God that He was the king and whatever He wanted was OK with us, but if He wouldn't mind, we'd like His help on a big problem.

JC: *Then* you had your strategy session.

KJ: No.

JC: What did you do?

KJ: We stood before God.

JC: Who did?

KJ: All of us. The men. The women. The babies. We just stood there and waited.

JC: What was the enemy doing while you were waiting?

KJ: They were getting closer.

JC: Is that when you rallied the people?

KJ: Who told you I rallied the people?

JC: Well, I just assumed . . .

KJ: I never said anything to the people. I just listened. After a while this young fellow named Jahaziel spoke up and said the Lord said not to be discouraged or afraid because the battle wasn't ours, it was His.

JC: How did you know He was speaking for God?

KJ: When you spend as much time talking to God as I do, you learn to recognise His voice.

JC: Incredible.

KJ: No, supernatural.

JC: Then you attacked?

KJ: No, Jahaziel said, 'Stand still and you will see the Lord save you.'

JC: I've heard that somewhere.

KJ: Vintage Moses.

JC: Then you attacked?

KJ: No, then we sang. Well, some sang. I'm not much

with a tune so I fell on my face and prayed. I let the others sing. We've got this group—Levites—who really know how to sing.

JC: Wait a minute. With the army getting closer, you sang?

KJ: A few tunes. Then I told the people to be strong and have faith in God and then we marched out to the battlefield.

JC: And you led the army?

KJ: No, we put the singers out in front. And as we marched they sang. And as we sang, God set ambushes. And by the time we got to the battlefield, the enemy was dead. That was three days ago. It took us that long to clean up the area. We are back today to have another worship service. Come over here; I want you to listen to these Levites sing. I bet you ten shekels you can't keep your seat for five minutes.

JC: Wait. I can't write this story. It's too bizarre. Who'll believe it?

KJ: Just write it. Those with man-sized problems will laugh. And those with God-sized problems will pray. Leave it to them to decide. Come on. The band is tuning up. You won't want to miss the first piece.

∞

So, what do you think? What does God do when we are in a bind? If Moses and Jehoshaphat are any indication, that question can be answered with one word: *fights*. He fights for us. He steps into the ring and points us to our corner and takes over. 'Remain calm; the LORD will fight for you' (Exod. 14:14).

His job is to fight. Our job is to trust.

Just trust. Not direct. Or question. Or yank the steering wheel out of His hands. Our job is to pray and wait. Nothing more is necessary. Nothing more is needed.

'He is my defender; I will not be defeated' (Ps. 62:6).

By the way, was it just me, or did I detect a few giggles when I announced my archaeological discovery?

Some of you didn't believe me, did you? Tsk, tsk, tsk . . . Just for that you're going to have to wait until the next book before I tell you about the diary of Jonah I found in a second-hand book store in Wink, Texas. Still has some whale guts in it.

And you thought I was kidding.[1]

PART THREE

The Guest
of the Maestro

What happens when a dog interrupts a concert? To answer that, come with me to a spring night in Lawrence, Kansas.

Take your seat in Hoch Auditorium and be-hold the Leipzig Gewandhaus Orchestra—the oldest continually operating orchestra in the world. The greatest composers and conductors in history have directed this orchestra. It was playing in the days of Beethoven (some of the musicians have been replaced).

You watch as Europeans in stately dress take their seats on the stage. You listen as professionals carefully tune their instruments. The percussionist puts her ear to the kettle drum. A violinist plucks the nylon sting. A clarinet player tightens the reed. And you sit a bit straighter as the lights dim and the tuning stops. The music is about to begin.

The conductor, dressed in tails, strides onto the stage, springs onto the podium, and gestures for the orchestra to rise. You and two thousand others applaud. The musicians take their seats, the maestro takes his position, and the audience holds its breath.

There is a second of silence between lightning and thunder. And there is a second of silence between the raising of the baton and the explosion of the music. But when it falls the heavens open and you are delightfully drenched in the downpour of Beethoven's Third Symphony.

Such was the power of that spring night in Lawrence, Kansas. That hot, spring night in Lawrence, Kansas. I mention the temperature so you'll understand why the doors were open. It was hot. Hoch Auditorium, a historic building,

*was not air-conditioned. Combine bright stage lights with
formal dress and furious music, and the result is a heated orchestra. Outside doors on each side of the stage were left
open in case of a breeze.*

*Enter, stage right, the dog. A brown, generic, Kansas dog.
Not a mean dog. Not a mad dog. Just a curious dog. He
passes between the double basses and makes his way through
the second violins and into the cellos. His tail wags in beat
with the music. As the dog passes between the players, they
look at him, look at each other, and continue with the next
measure.*

*The dog takes a liking to a certain cello. Perhaps it was
the lateral passing of the bow. Maybe it was the eye-level
view of the strings. Whatever it was, it caught the dog's attention and he stopped and watched. The cellist wasn't sure
what to do. He'd never played before a canine audience. And
music schools don't teach you what dog slobber might do to
the lacquer of a sixteenth-century Guarneri cello. But the
dog did nothing but watch for a moment and then move on.*

*Had he passed on through the orchestra, the music might
have continued. Had he made his way across the stage into
the motioning hands of the stagehand, the audience might
never have noticed. But he didn't leave. He stayed. At home
in the splendour. Roaming through the meadow of music.*

*He visited the woodwinds, turned his head at the trum-
pets, stepped between the flautists, and stopped by the side
of the conductor. And Beethoven's Third Symphony came
undone.*

*The musicians laughed. The audience laughed. The dog
looked up at the conductor and panted. And the conductor
lowered his baton.*

*The most historic orchestra in the world. One of the most
moving pieces ever written. A night wrapped in glory, all
brought to a stop by a wayward dog.*

The chuckles ceased as the conductor turned. What fury might erupt? The audience grew quiet as the maestro faced them. What fuse had been lit? The polished, German director looked at the crowd, looked down at the dog, then looked back at the people, raised his hands in a universal gesture and . . . shrugged.

Everyone roared.

He stepped off the podium and scratched the dog behind the ears. The tail wagged again. The maestro spoke to the dog. He spoke in German, but the dog seemed to understand. The two enjoyed each other's company for a few seconds before the maestro took his new friend by the collar and led him off the stage. You'd have thought the dog was Pavarotti the way the people applauded. The conductor returned and the music began and Beethoven seemed none the worse for the whole experience.[1]

Can you find you and me in this picture?

I can. Just call us Fido. And consider God the Maestro.

And envision the moment when we will walk onto His stage. We won't deserve it. We will not have earned it. We may even surprise the musicians with our presence.

The music will be like none we've ever heard. We'll stroll among the angels and listen as they sing. We'll gaze at heaven's lights and gasp as they shine. And we'll walk next to the Maestro, stand by His side, and worship as He leads.

These final chapters remind us of that moment. They challenge us to see the unseen and live for that event. They invite us to tune our ears to the song of the skies and long— long for the moment when we'll be at the Maestro's side.

He, too, will welcome. And He, too, will speak. But He will not lead us away. He will invite us to remain, forever His guests on His stage.

CHAPTER TWENTY-FOUR

The Gift of Unhappiness

There dwells inside you, deep within, a tiny songird. Listen. You will hear him sing. His aria mourns the dusk. His solo signals the dawn.

He will not be silent until the sun is seen.

We forget he is there, so easy is he to ignore. Other animals of the heart are larger, noisier, more demanding, more imposing.

But none is so constant.

Other creatures of the soul are more quickly fed. More simply satisfied. We feed the lion who growls for power. We stroke the tiger who demands affection. We bridle the stallion who bucks control.

But what do we do with the little bird who yearns for eternity?

For that is his song. That is his task. Out of the grey he sings a golden song. Perched in time he chirps a timeless verse. Peering through pain's shroud, he sees a painless place. Of that place he sings.

And though we try to ignore him, we cannot. He is us,

and his song is ours. Our heart song won't be silenced until we see the dawn.

'God has planted eternity in the hearts of men' (Eccles. 3:10 TLB), says the wise man. But it doesn't take a wise person to know that people long for more than earth. When we see pain, we yearn. When we see hunger, we question why. Senseless deaths. Endless tears, needless loss. Where do they come from? Where will they lead?

Isn't there more to life than death?

And so sings the tiny bird.

We try to quiet this terrible, tiny voice. Like a parent hushing a child, we place a finger over puckered lips and request silence. *I'm too busy now to talk. I'm too busy to think. I'm too busy to question.*

And so we busy ourselves with the task of staying busy.

But occasionally we hear his song. And occasionally we let the song whisper to us that there is something more. There *must* be something more.

And as long as we hear the song, we are comforted. As long as we are discontented, we will search. As long as we know there is a far-off country, we will have hope.

The only ultimate disaster that can befall us, I have come to realise, is to feel ourselves to be home on earth. As long as we are aliens, we cannot forget our true homeland.[1]

Unhappiness on earth cultivates a hunger for heaven. By gracing us with a deep dissatisfaction, God holds our attention. The only tragedy, then, is to be satisfied prematurely. To settle for earth. To be content in a strange land. To intermarry with the Babylonians and forget Jerusalem.

We are not happy here because we are not at home here. We are not happy here because we are not supposed to be happy here. We are 'like foreigners and strangers in this world" (1 Pet. 2:11).

Take a fish and place him on the beach.[2] Watch his gills

gasp and scales dry. Is he happy? No! How do you make him happy? Do you cover him with a mountain of cash? Do you get him a beach chair and sunglasses? Do you bring him a *Playfish* magazine and martini? Do you wardrobe him in double-breasted fins and people-skinned shoes?

Of course not. Then how do you make him happy? You put him back in his element. You put him back in the water. He will never be happy on the beach simply because he was not made for the beach.

And you will never be completely happy on earth simply because you were not made for earth. Oh, you will have your moments of joy. You will catch glimpses of light. You will know moments or even days of peace. But they simply do not compare with the happiness that lies ahead.

Thou hast made us for thyself and our hearts are restless until they rest in thee.[3]

Rest on this earth is a false rest. Beware of those who urge you to find happiness here; you won't find it. Guard against the false physicians who promise that joy is only a diet away, a marriage away, a job away, or a transfer away. The prophet denounced people like this, 'They tried to heal my people's serious injuries as if they were small wounds. They said, "It's all right, it's all right." But really, it is not all right' (Jer. 6:14).

And it won't be all right until we get home.

Again, we have our moments. The newborn on our breast, the bride on our arm, the sunshine on our back. But even those moments are simply slivers of light breaking through heaven's window. God flirts with us. He tantalises us. He romances us. Those moments are appetisers for the dish that is to come.

'No one has ever imagined what God has prepared for those who love him' (1 Cor. 2:9).

What a breathtaking verse! Do you see what it says? *Heaven is beyond our imagination*. We cannot envision it. At our most creative moment, at our deepest thought, at our highest level, we still cannot fathom eternity.

Try this. Imagine a perfect world. Whatever that means to you, imagine it. Does that mean peace? Then envision absolute tranquillity. Does a perfect world imply joy? Then create your highest happiness. Will a perfect world have love? If so, ponder a place where love has no bounds. Whatever heaven means to you, imagine it. Get it firmly fixed in your mind. Delight in it. Dream about it. Long for it.

And then smile as the Father reminds you, *No one has ever imagined what God has prepared for those who love Him.*

Anything you imagine is inadequate. Anything anyone imagines is inadequate. No one has come close. No one. Think of all the songs about heaven. All the artists' portrayals. All the lessons preached, poems written, and chapters drafted.

When it comes to describing heaven, we are all happy failures.

It's beyond us.

But it's also within us. The song of the whippoorwill. Let her sing. Let her sing in the dark. Let her sing at the dawn. Let her song remind you that you were not made for this place and that there is a place made just for you.

But until then, be realistic. Lower your expectations of earth. This is not heaven, so don't expect it to be. There will never be a news bulletin with no bad news. There will never be a church with no gossip or competition. There will never be a new car, new wife, or new baby who can give you the joy your heart craves. Only God can.

And God will. Be patient. And be listening. Listening for the little bird's song.

CHAPTER TWENTY-FIVE

On Seeing God

One of my favourite childhood memories is greeting my father as he came home from work.

My mother, who worked an evening shift at the hospital, would leave the house around three in the afternoon. Dad would arrive home at three-thirty. My brother and I were left alone for that half-hour with strict instructions not to leave the house until Dad arrived.

We would take our positions on the sofa and watch cartoons, always keeping one ear alert to the drive. Even the best 'Daffy Duck' would be abandoned when we heard his car.

I can remember running out to meet Dad and getting swept up in his big (often sweaty) arms. As he carried me toward the house, he'd put his big-brimmed straw hat on my head, and for a moment I'd be a cowboy. We'd sit on the porch as he removed his oily work boots (never allowed in the house). As he took them off I'd pull them on, and for a moment I'd be a wrangler. Then we'd go indoors and open his lunch box. Any leftover snacks, which he always seemed to have, were for my brother and me to share.

It was great. Boots, hats, and snacks. What more could a five-year-old want?

But suppose, for a minute, that is all I got. Suppose my dad, rather than coming home, just sent some things home. Boots for me to play in. A hat for me to wear. Snacks for me to eat.

Would that be enough? Maybe so, but not for long. Soon the gifts would lose their charm. Soon, if not immediately, I'd ask, 'Where's Dad?'

Or consider something worse. Suppose he called me up and said, 'Max, I won't be coming home any more. But I'll send my boots and hat over, and every afternoon you can play in them.'

No deal. That wouldn't work. Even a five-year-old knows it's the person, not the presents, that makes a reunion special. It's not the frills; it's the father.

Imagine God making us a similar offer:

I will give you anything you desire. Anything. Perfect love. Eternal peace. You will never be afraid or alone. No confusion will enter your mind. No anxiety or boredom will enter your heart. You will never lack for anything.

There will be no sin. No guilt. No rules. No expectations. No failure. You will never be lonely. You will never hurt. You will never die.

Only you will never see my face.[1]

Would you want it? Neither would I. It's not enough. Who wants heaven without God? Heaven is not heaven without God.

A painless, deathless eternity will be nice, but inadequate. A world shot with splendour would stagger us, but it's not what we seek. What we want is God. We want God more than we know. It's not that the perks aren't attractive. It's just that they aren't enough. It's not that we are greedy. It's just that we are His and—Augustine was right—our hearts are restless until they rest in Him.

Only when we find Him will we be satisfied. Moses can tell you.

He had as much of God as any man in the Bible. God spoke to him in a bush. God guided him with fire. God amazed Moses with the plagues. And when God grew angry with the Israelites and withdrew from them, He stayed close to Moses. He spoke to Moses 'as a man speaks with his friend" (Exod. 33:11). Moses knew God like no other man.

But that wasn't enough. Moses yearned for more. Moses longed to see God. He even dared to ask, 'Please show me your glory" (Exod. 33:18).

A hat and snack were not enough. A fiery pillar and morning manna were insufficient. Moses wanted to see God himself.

Don't we all?

Isn't that why we long for heaven? We may speak about a place where there are no tears, no death, no fear, no night; but those are just the benefits of heaven. The beauty of heaven is seeing God. Heaven is God's heart.

And our heart will only be at peace when we see Him. 'Because I have lived right, I will see your face. When I wake up, I will see your likeness and be satisfied" (Ps. 17:15).

Satisfied? That is one thing we are not. We are not satisfied.

We push back from the Thanksgiving table and pat our round bellies. 'I'm satisfied,' we declare. But look at us a few hours later, back in the kitchen picking the meat from the bone.

We wake up after a good night's rest and hop out of bed. We couldn't go back to sleep if someone paid us. We are satisfied—for a while. But look at us a dozen or so hours later, crawling back in the sheets.

We take the holiday of a lifetime. For years we planned. For years we saved. And off we go. We satiate ourselves with sun, fun, and good food. But we are not even on the way home before we dread the end of the trip and begin planning another.

We are not satisfied.

As a child we say, 'If only I were a teenager.' As a teen we say, 'If only I were an adult.' As an adult, 'If only I were married.' As a spouse, 'If only I had kids.' As a parent, 'If only my kids were grown up.' In an empty house, 'If only the kids would visit.' As a retiree in the rocking chair with stiff joints and fading sight, 'If only I were a child again.'

We are not satisfied. Contentment is a difficult virtue. Why?

Because there is nothing on earth that can satisfy our deepest longing. We long to see God. The leaves of life are rustling with the rumour that we will—and we won't be satisfied until we do.

We can't be satisfied. Not because we are greedy, but because we are hungry for something not found on this earth. Only God can satisfy. Philip was right when he said, 'Lord, show us the Father. That is all we need" (John 14:8).

Alas, therein lies the problem: 'But you cannot see my face,' God told Moses, 'because no one can see me and live" (Exod. 33:20).

The eighteenth-century *Hasids* understood the risk of seeing God. Rabbi Uri wept every morning as he left his house to pray. He called his children and wife to his side and wept as if he would never see them again. When asked why, he gave this answer. 'When I begin my prayers I call out to the Lord. Then I pray, 'Lord have mercy on us.' Who knows what the Lord's power will do to me in that moment after I have invoked it and before I beg for mercy?'[2]

According to legend, the first American Indian to see the Grand Canyon tied himself to a tree in terror. According to Scripture, any man privileged with a peek at God has felt the same.

Sheer terror. Remember the words of Isaiah after his vision of God? 'Oh, no! I will be destroyed. I am not pure, and I live among people who are not pure, but I have seen the King, the LORD All-Powerful" (Isa. 6:5).

Upon seeing God, Isaiah was terrified. Why such fear? Why did he tremble so? Because he was wax before the sun. A candle in a hurricane. A minnow at Niagara. God's glory was too great. His purity too sterling. His power too mighty.

The holiness of God illuminates the sinfulness of man.

To understand this, let's imagine you are in a theatre. You have never visited one before and you are curious. You poke around backstage and look at the lights and play with the curtains and examine the props. Then you see a dressing room.

You enter and sit at the table. You look in the large mirror on the wall. What you see is what you always see when you look at your reflection. No surprises. Then you notice that the mirror is framed in light bulbs. There is a switch on the wall. You flip it on.

A dozen lights shine on your face. Suddenly you see what you had not seen. Blemishes. Wrinkles. Every mole and mark is highlighted. The light has illuminated your imperfections.

That's what happened to Isaiah. When he saw God, he didn't sigh with admiration. He didn't applaud in appreciation. He drew back in horror, crying, 'I am unclean and my people are unclean!'

The holiness of God highlights our sins.

Listen to the words of another prophet. 'Look, Jesus is coming with the clouds, and everyone will see him, even those who stabbed him. And all peoples of the earth will *cry loudly* because of him. Yes, this will happen!' (Rev. 1:7, emphasis mine).

Read the verse in another translation. 'Riding the clouds, he'll be seen by every eye, those who mocked and killed him will see him. People from all nations and all times will tear their clothes in lament. Oh, yes' (Rev. 1:7, THE MESSAGE).

The holiness of God highlights the sin of man.

Then what do we do? If it is true that 'Anyone whose life is not holy will never see the Lord' (Heb. 12:14), where do we turn?

We can't turn off the light. We can't flip the switch. We can't return to the grey. By then it will be too late.

So what can we do?

The answer is found in the story of Moses. Read carefully, very carefully, the following verses. Read to answer this question—what did Moses do in order to see God? Read slowly what God says. You may miss it.

'There is a place near me where you may stand on a rock. When my glory passes that place, I will put you in a large crack in the rock and cover you with my hand until I have passed by. Then I will take away my hand, and you will see my back. But my face must not be seen' (Exod. 33:21–23).

Did you see what Moses was to do? Neither did I. Did you note who did the work? So did I.

God did! God is active. God gave Moses a place to stand. God placed Moses in the crevice. God covered Moses with His hand. God passed by. And God revealed Himself.

Please, underscore the point. God equipped Moses to catch a glimpse of God.

(*Holy Moses!*)

All Moses did was ask. But, oh, how he asked.

All we can do is ask. But, oh, we must ask.

For only in asking do we receive. And only in seeking do we find.

And (need I make the application?) God is the One who will equip us for our eternal moment in the Son. Hasn't He given us a rock, the Lord Jesus? Hasn't He given us a cleft, His grace? And hasn't He covered us with His hand, His pierced hand?

And isn't the Father on His way to get us?

Just as my dad came at the right hour, so God will come. And just as my father brought gifts and pleasures, so will yours. But, as splendid as are the gifts of heaven, it is not for those we wait.

We wait to see the Father. And that will be enough.

CHAPTER TWENTY-SIX

Orphans at the Gate

I came across a sad story this week, a story about a honeymoon disaster. The newlyweds arrived at the hotel in the wee hours with high hopes. They'd reserved a large room with romantic amenities. That's not what they found.

Seems the room was pretty skimpy. The tiny room had no view, no flowers, a cramped bathroom and worst of all—no bed. Just a foldout sofa with a lumpy mattress and sagging springs. It was not what they'd hoped for; consequently, neither was the night.

The next morning the sore-necked groom stormed down to the manager's desk and vented his anger. After listening patiently for a few minutes, the clerk asked, 'Did you open the door in your room?'

The groom admitted he hadn't. He returned to the suite and opened the door he had thought was a cupboard. There, complete with fruit baskets and chocolates, was a spacious bedroom![1]

Sigh.

Can't you just see them standing in the doorway of the room they'd overlooked? Oh, it would have been so nice . . .

A comfortable bed instead of a lumpy sofa.

A curtain-framed window rather than a blank wall.

A fresh breeze in place of stuffy air.

An elaborate bathroom, not a tight toilet.

But they missed it. How sad. Cramped, cranky, and uncomfortable while comfort was a door away. They missed it because they thought the door was a cupboard.

Why didn't you try? I was asking as I read the piece. Get curious. Check it out. Give it a shot. Take a look. Why did you just assume the door led nowhere?

Good question. Not just for the couple but for everyone. Not for the pair who thought the room was all there was, but for all who feel cramped and packed in the anteroom called earth. It's not what we'd hoped. It may have its moments, but it is simply not what we think it should be. Something inside of us groans for more.

We understand what Paul meant when he wrote: 'We . . . groan inwardly as we wait eagerly our adoption as sons, the redemption of our bodies' (Rom. 8:23 NIV).

Groan. That's the word. An inward *angst*. The echo from the cavern of the heart. The sigh of the soul that says the world is out of joint. Awry. Misspelled. Limping.

Something is wrong.

The room is too cramped to breathe, the bed too stiff for rest, the walls too bare for pleasure.

And so we groan.

It's not that we don't try. We do our best with the room we have. We shuffle the furniture, we paint the walls, we turn down the lights. But there's only so much you can do with the place.

And so we groan.

And well we should, Paul argues. We were not made for these puny quarters. 'For while we are in this tent, we groan and are burdened' (2 Cor. 5:6).

Our body a tent? Not a bad metaphor. I've spent some nights in tents. Nice for holidays, but not intended for daily use. Flaps fly open. Winter wind creeps from beneath. Summer showers seep from above. Canvas gets raw and tent stakes come loose.

We need something better, Paul argues. Something permanent. Something painless. Something more than flesh and bone. And until we get it, we groan.

I know I'm not telling you anything new. You know the groan of the soul. You didn't need me to tell you it's there.

But maybe you do need me to tell you it's OK. It's all right to groan. It's permissible to yearn. Longing is part of life. It's only natural to long for home when on a journey.

We aren't home yet.

We are orphans at the gate of the orphanage, awaiting our new parents. They aren't here yet, but we know they are coming. They wrote us a letter. We haven't seen them yet, but we know what they look like. They sent us a picture. And we're not acquainted with our new house yet, but we have a hunch about it. It's grand. They sent a description.

And so what do we do? Here, at the gate where the now-already meets the path of the not-yet, what do we do?

We groan. We long for the call to come home. But until He calls, we wait. We stand on the porch of the orphanage and wait. And how do we wait? With patient eagerness.

'We are hoping for something we do not have yet, and we are waiting for it *patiently*' (Rom. 8:25, emphasis mine).

'We wait *eagerly* for our adoption as sons' (Rom. 8:23 NIV, emphasis mine). Patient eagerness. Not so eager as to lose our patience, and not so patient as to lose our eagerness.[2]

Yet, we often tend to one or the other.

We grow so patient we sleep! Our eyelids grow heavy. Our hearts grow drowsy. Our hope lapses. We slumber at our post.

Or we are so eager we demand. We demand in this world what only the next world can give. No sickness. No suffering. No struggle. We stomp our feet and shake our fists, forgetting it is only in heaven that such peace is found.

We must be patient, but not so much that we don't yearn. We must be eager, but not so much that we don't wait.

We'd be wise to do what the newlyweds never did. We'd be wise to open the door. Stand in the entryway. Gaze in the chambers. Gasp at the beauty.

And wait. Wait for the groom to come and carry us, His bride, over the threshold.

CHAPTER TWENTY-SEVEN

View of the High Country

While in Colorado for a week's holiday, our family teamed up with several others and decided to ascend the summit of a fourteen-thousand-foot peak. We would climb it the easy way. Drive above the timberline and tackle the final mile by foot. You hearty hikers would have been bored, but for a family with three small girls, it was about all we could take.

The journey was as tiring as it was beautiful. I was reminded how the air was thin and my waist was not.

Our four-year-old Sara had it doubly difficult. A tumble in the first few minutes left her with a skinned knee and a timid step. She didn't want to walk. Actually, she *refused* to walk. She wanted to ride. First on my back, then in Mum's arms, then my back, then a friend's back, then my back, then Mum's . . . well, you get the picture.

In fact, you know how she felt. You, too, have tumbled, and you, too, have asked for help. And you, too, have received it.

All of us need help sometimes. This journey gets steep. So steep that some of us give up.

Some stop climbing. Some just sit down. They are still near the trail but aren't on it. They haven't abandoned the trip, but they haven't continued it. They haven't dismounted, but they haven't spurred either. They haven't resigned and yet haven't resolved.

They have simply stopped walking. Much time is spent sitting around the fire, talking about how things used to be. Some will sit in the same place for years. They will not change. Prayers will not deepen. Devotion will not increase. Passion will not rise.

A few even grow cynical. Woe to the traveller who challenges them to resume the journey. Woe to the prophet who dares them to see the mountain. Woe to the explorer who reminds them of their call . . . pilgrims are not welcome here.

And so the pilgrim moves on while the settler settles.

Settles for sameness.

Settles for safety.

Settles for snowdrifts.

I hope you don't do that. But if you do, I hope you don't scorn the pilgrim who calls you back to the journey.

It's worth it to keep moving.

As I tried, unsuccessfully, to convince Sara to walk, I tried describing what we were going to see. 'It will be so pretty,' I told her. 'You'll see all the mountains and the sky and the trees.' No luck—she wanted to be carried. Still a good idea, however. Even if it didn't work. Nothing puts power in the journey like a vision of the mountaintop.

By the way, a grand scene awaits you as well. The Hebrew writer gives us a *National Geographic* piece on heaven. Listen to how he describes the mountaintop of Zion. He says when we reach the mountain we will have come to 'the city of the living God . . . to thousands of angels gathered together with joy . . . to the meeting of God's firstborn children whose names are written in heaven . . . to God, the judge of all people, . . . and to the spirits of good people who have been made perfect . . . to Jesus, the One who brought the new agreement from God to His people . . . to the sprinkled blood that has a better message than the blood of Abel" (Heb. 12:22–24).

What a mountain! Won't it be great to see the angels? To finally know what they look like and who they are? To hear them tell of the times they were at our side, even in our house?

Imagine the meeting of the firstborn. A gathering of all God's children. No jealousy. No competition. No division. No hurry. We will be perfect . . . sinless. No more stumbles. No more tripping. Lusting will cease. Gossip will be silenced. Grudges forever removed.

And imagine seeing God. Finally, to gaze in the face of your Father. To feel the Father's gaze upon you. Neither will ever cease.

He will do what He promised He would do. *I will make all things new,* He promised. *I will restore what was taken. I will restore your years drooped on crutches and trapped in wheelchairs. I will restore the smiles faded by hurt. I will replay the symphonies unheard by deaf ears and the sunsets unseen by blind eyes.*

The mute will sing. The poor will feast. The wounds will heal.

I will make all things new. I will restore all things. The child snatched by disease will run to your arms. The freedom lost to oppression will dance in your heart. The peace of a pure heart will be my gift to you.

I will make all things new. New hope. New faith. And most of all new Love. The Love of which all other loves speak. The Love before which all other loves pale. The Love you have sought in a thousand ports in a thousand nights . . . this Love of mine, will be yours.[1]

What a mountain! Jesus will be there. You've longed to see Him. You finally will. Interesting what the writer says we will see. He doesn't mention the face of Jesus, though we will see it. He doesn't refer to the voice of Jesus, though it will shout. He mentions a part of Jesus that most of us wouldn't think of seeing. He says we will see Jesus' blood. The crimson of the cross. The life liquid that seeped from His forehead, dripped from His hands, and flowed from His side.

The human blood of the divine Christ. Covering our sins.

Proclaiming a message: *We have been bought. We cannot be sold. Ever.*

My, what a moment. What a mountain.

Believe me when I say it will be worth it. No cost is too high. If you must pay a price, pay it! No sacrifice too much. If you must leave baggage on the trail, leave it! No loss will compare. Whatever it takes, do it.

For heaven's sake, do it.

It will be worth it. I promise. One view of the peak will justify the pain of the path.

By the way, our group finally made it up the mountain. We spent an hour or so at the top, taking pictures and enjoying the view. Later, on the way down, I heard little Sara exclaim proudly, 'I did it!'

I chuckled. *No you didn't,* I thought. *Your mum and I did it. Friends and family got you up this mountain. You didn't do it.*

But I didn't say anything. I didn't say anything because I'm getting the same treatment. So are you. We may think we are climbing, but we are riding. Riding on the back of the Father who saw us fall. Riding on the back of the Father who wants us to make it home. A Father who doesn't get angry when we get weary.

After all, He knows what it's like to climb a mountain.

He climbed one for us.

CHAPTER TWENTY-EIGHT

The Name Only God Knows

Had a picture given to me after a church service sometime back. A picture of a dog. A snapshot of a scruffy red hound.

It's not often that people show me a picture of their dog. Babies, yes. Grandchildren, often. Spouses, occasionally. But dogs? This was a first. I didn't know what to say.

'Quite a dog,' I attempted. The couple looked at each other, sniggered, and looked back at me. They knew something I didn't.

'What's the scoop?' I asked. (Poor choice of nouns.)

'We named him Max!' they proclaimed in unison.

Again I was stumped. Was this a joke or an honour? A cut or a compliment?

I took the safe route. 'Uh . . . I've never had a dog named after me before.'

'We knew you'd be flattered,' she explained. 'We've enjoyed your books so much that when we got "Puppy-boo" we thought of you.'

(*Puppy-boo?*)

I said thanks and pocketed the photo. Only later did I

think of some appropriate replies. 'Not the first Max to be in a doghouse,' was one. Too bad I didn't think of it in time. A friend later gave me an article reporting that Max is the most popular name for dogs in America. So maybe I'll get another chance.

Can't say I've given a lot of thought to my given name. Never figured it made much difference. I do recall a kid in elementary school wondering if I were German. I said no. 'Then why do you have a German name?' I didn't even know Max was German. He assured me it was. So I decided to find out.

'Why did you name me Max?' I asked Mum when I got home.

She looked up from the sink and replied, 'You just looked like one.'

As I say, I haven't given much thought to my name. But there is one name that has caught my interest lately. A name only God knows. A name only God gives. A unique, one-of-a-kind, once-to-be-given name.

What am I talking about? Well, you may not have known it, but God has a new name for you. When you get home, He won't call you Alice or Bob or Juan or Geraldo. The name you've always heard won't be the one He uses. When God says He will make all things new, He means it. You will have a new home, a new body, a new life, and you guessed it, a new name.

'I will give some of the hidden manna to everyone who wins the victory. I will also give to each one who wins the victory a white stone with a new name written on it. No one knows this new name except the one who receives it" (Rev. 2:17).

Makes sense. Fathers are fond of giving their children special names. Princess. Tiger. Sweetheart. Bubba. Angel. I have a friend whose father calls her Willy. Her name is Priscilla. Growing up, he teased her by saying Priscilly. That became Silly-willy. Today he calls her Willy. No one else does. Even if they did, no one else could say it the way her dad does.

Now maybe you didn't get a special name. Or maybe you've devoted much of your life to making a name for yourself. Or perhaps your name, like mine, is popular in the animal kingdom. Whatever, any earthly name will soon be forgotten. The only name that matters is the one God has reserved just for you.

Or maybe you have received special names. Names you never sought. Names of derision and hurt. Names like 'loser" or 'cheat', 'cripple', 'infected', or 'divorced'. If so, I'm sorry. You know how a name can hurt. But you can also imagine how a name can heal.

Especially when it comes from the lips of God.

Isn't it incredible to think that God has saved a name just for you? One you don't even know? We've always assumed that the name we got is the name we will keep. Not so. Imagine what that implies. Apparently your future is so promising it warrants a new title. The road ahead is so bright a fresh name is needed. Your eternity is so special no common name will do.

So God has one reserved just for you. There is more to your life than you ever thought. There is more to your story than what you have read. There is more to your song than what you have sung. A good author saves the best for last. A great composer keeps his finest for the finish. And God, the author of life and composer of hope, has done the same for you.

The best is yet to be.

And so I urge you, don't give up.

And so I plead, finish the journey.

And so I exhort, be there.

Be there when God whispers your name.

NOTES

CHAPTER 1 The Voice from the Mop Bucket
1. Philippians 1:6.

CHAPTER 3 Hidden Heroes
1. See Matthew 11:2.
2. *1,041 Sermon Illustrations, Ideas and Expositions*, compiled and edited by A. Gordon Nasby (Grand Rapids: Baker, 1976), 180–81.

CHAPTER 7 Behind the Shower Curtain
1. These phrases appeared in 'A Dream Worth Keeping Alive,' *Wineskins Magazine*, January–February 1993, 16–20.
2. See Luke 15:3–7.

CHAPTER 9 What Is Your Price?
1. James Patterson and Peter Kim, *The Day America Told the Truth* (New York: Prentice Hall, 1991), as quoted in *Discipleship Journal*, September—October 1991, 16.
2. Ibid.
3. 'Life is not measured by how much one owns" (Luke 12:15).
4. Better known as the Parable of Greed (Luke 12:16–21).

PART 2 The Touch of the Master
1. *1041 Sermon Illustrations, Ideas, and Expositions,* 199.

CHAPTER 15 Overcoming Your Heritage
1. With appreciation to Stefan Richart-Willmes.

CHAPTER 23 The God Who Fights for You
1. See Exodus 14:5–31, Exodus chapters 8–15, and 2 Chronicles 20.

PART 3 The Guest of the Maestro
1. With appreciation to Erik Ketcherside for telling me this story.

CHAPTER 24 The Gift of Unhappiness
1. Augustine, *Confessions I.i,* as quoted in Peter Kreeft, *Heaven: The Heart's Deepest Longing* (San Francisco: Ignatius Press), 1989, 49. The inspiration for this essay about the song bird is drawn from Kreeft's description of 'The Nightingale in the Heart,' 51–54.
2. With appreciation to Landon Saunders for this idea.
3. Malcolm Muggeridge, *Jesus Rediscovered* (New York: Doubleday, 1979), 47–48 as quoted in Peter Kreeft, *Heaven,* 63.

CHAPTER 25 On Seeing God
1. With acknowledgement to Augustine, *Ennarationes in Psalmos,* 127.9, as quoted in Peter Kreeft, *Heaven,* 49.
2. Annie Dillard, *The Writing Life* (New York: Harper and Row, 1989), 9.

CHAPTER 26 Orphans at the Gate

1.   *Leadership*, Winter 1994, 46.
2.   With appreciation to John R. W. Stott, *Christian Assurance: The Hope of Glory* (London: All Souls Cassettes), d28 1b.

CHAPTER 27 View of the High Country

1.   See Revelation 21:5.

DISCUSSION GUIDE

Prepared by
Steve Halliday

HOW TO USE THIS DISCUSSION GUIDE

Each of these short studies is designed not only to interact with the ideas in *When God Whispers Your Name*, but also to point readers back to Scripture as the wellspring of those ideas.

The first section of each study, Points to Ponder, excerpts portions of each chapter for group discussion. The second section, Wisdom from the Word, helps readers dig a little deeper into the scriptural viewpoint on the issue under discussion.

While all of the studies may be completed separately, they may also be considered together with one or more other studies that cover similar themes. A suggested list of complementary studies follows:

- The Voice From the Mop Bucket/Hidden Heroes/You Might've Been in the Bible
- Why Jesus Went to Parties/Maxims
- Behind the Shower Curtain/Groceries and Grace/Of Oz and God

CHAPTER 1   THE VOICE FROM THE MOP BUCKET

Points to Ponder

'Something happens to us along the way. Convictions to change the world downgrade to commitments to pay the bills. Rather than make a difference, we make a salary. Rather than look forward, we look back. Rather than look outward, we look inward. And we don't like what we see.'

1   Have your convictions changed as you've grown older? If so, in what way?

2   Do you like what you see? Explain.

'Moses at forty we like. But Moses at eighty? No way. Too old. Too tired. Smells like a shepherd. Speaks like a foreigner. What impact would he have on Pharaoh? He's the wrong man for the job. Moses would have agreed. "Tried that once before," he would say. "Those people don't want to be helped. Just leave me here to tend my sheep. They're easier to lead." Moses wouldn't have gone. You wouldn't have sent him. I wouldn't have sent him. But God did.'

1   Would you have given Moses the job of bringing Israel out of slavery? Explain.

2   What do you think God saw in Moses? What do you think He might see in you?

'The voice from the bush reminds you that God is not finished with you yet. Oh, you may think He is. You may think you've peaked. You may think He's got someone else to do the job. If so, think again.'

1   How does the 'voice from the bush" remind you that God isn't finished with you yet?

2   Have you ever had a 'burning bush" experience? If so, describe it.

3   What do you think God may still be calling you to do?

Wisdom from the Word

🌱   Read Exodus 6:28–7:6. What did Moses think of himself? What did God think of him? Whose opinion won out?

🌱   Read Hebrews 11:24–28. According to this passage, how did Moses accomplish what he did? How does this relate to you?

🌱   Read Philippians 1:6. What promise is given in this verse? How can it change the way you live? Does it affect the way you live personally? Explain.

∞

CHAPTER 2   WHY JESUS WENT TO PARTIES

Points to Ponder

'I think it's significant that common folk in a little town enjoyed being with Jesus. I think it's noteworthy that the Almighty didn't act high and mighty. The Holy One wasn't holier-than-thou. The One who knew it all wasn't a know-all. The One who made the stars didn't keep his head in them. The One who owns all the stuff of earth never strutted it.'

1   Is it important to you that the 'common folk' enjoyed being around Jesus? Explain.

2   Use a single word to describe the trait in Jesus' life that's described above.

'Where did we get the notion that a good Christian is a solemn Christian? Who started the rumor that the sign of a disciple is a long face? How did we create this idea that the truly gifted are the heavy-hearted?'

1   Do you think of Christians as 'solemn'? Explain.

2   Where do you think the idea of the heavy-hearted Christian came from?

3   Would others see you as a disciple with a long face? Explain.

'Forgive me, Deacon Drydust and Sister Sombreheart. I'm sorry to rain on your dirge, but Jesus was a likeable fellow. And His disciples should be the same. I'm not talking debauchery, drunkenness, and adultery. I'm not endorsing compromise, coarseness, or obscenity. I am simply crusading for the freedom to enjoy a good joke, enliven a dull party, and appreciate a fun evening.'

1   Describe your response to Max's insight above.

2   How do you respond to the Deacon Drydusts and Sister Sombrehearts you encounter? How do you think Jesus would respond to them?

Wisdom from the Word

🌢   Read John 2:1–11. What impression do you get of Jesus from this passage? Why do you think John included it in his Gospel?

🌢   Read Matthew 11:18–19. Which parts of this accusation against Jesus are true, and which are false? What does this passage tell you about Jesus' lifestyle? How does this relate to Max's point?

🌢   Read 1 Thessalonians 4:16. What does it mean to 'rejoice"? Why is it significant that this is a command? How good are you at obeying this command?

CHAPTER 3   HIDDEN HEROES

Points to Ponder

'John doesn't look like the prophet who would be the transition between law and grace. He doesn't look like a hero. Heroes seldom do.'

1   In what way do heroes seldom look like heroes?

2   What's your picture of a hero?

'For every hero in the spotlight, there are dozens in the shadows. They don't get press. They don't draw crowds. They don't even write books (!). But behind every avalanche is a snowflake. Behind a rock slide is a pebble. An atomic explosion begins with one atom. And a revival can begin with one sermon.'

1   What 'heroes out of the spotlight" do you know?

2   What makes them heroes?

'We'd do well to keep our eyes open. Tomorrow's Spurgeon might be mowing your lawn. And the hero who inspires him might be nearer than you think. He might be in your mirror.'

1   Have you been a hero to anyone?

2   Could you be a hero to anyone?

Wisdom from the Word

🔖   Read Mark 1:1–8. How would you describe John in modern terms? How did his appearance and lifestyle help him accomplish his mission? In what way was he a hero?

🔖   Read 2 Corinthians 4:7–11; 6:4–10; 11:22–28. What do you learn about Paul from these passages? What in them describes the kind of hero he was? Do these passages encourage or discourage you? Why?

CHAPTER 4   YOU MIGHT'VE BEEN IN THE BIBLE

Points to Ponder

'In evangelism the Holy Spirit is on centre stage. If the

disciple teaches, it is because the Spirit teaches the disciple (Luke 12:12). If the listener is convicted, it is because the Spirit has penetrated (John 16:10). If the listener is converted, it is by the transforming power of the Spirit (Rom. 8:11).'

1   How have you seen the Holy Spirit at work in your own life in the process of evangelism?

2   What difference does it make to you that the Holy Spirit is at work alongside you in evangelism?

'You have the same Spirit working with you that Philip did. Some of you don't believe me. You're still cautious.'

1   How is the Spirit's working in your life the same as it was in Philip's? How is it different?

2   Are you one of the 'cautious' ones? Explain.

Wisdom from the Word

🍇   Read Acts 8:26–40. List the steps Philip took, directed by the Spirit. What principles of effective evangelism can you glean from this passage? Which ones do you use? Which ones don't you use? Explain.

🍇   Read Romans 8:13–14; Galatians 5:16–18. What do these passages teach about the leading of the Spirit? What is promised? What warnings are given?

∞

CHAPTER 5   MAXIMS

Points to Ponder

'We learn brevity from Jesus. His greatest sermon can be

read in eight minutes. His best-known story can be read in ninety seconds. He summarised prayer in five phrases. He silenced accusers with one challenge. He rescued a soul with one sentence. He summarised the Law in three verses and reduced all His teachings to one command. He made His point and went home.'

1   What is so powerful about brevity? What can make it so effective?

2   Which of Max's maxims in this chapter most struck a chord in you? Why?

Wisdom from the Word

- Read Luke 15:11–32. Why do you think this is Jesus' best-known story? What makes it so powerful?

- Read Matthew 6:9–13. List the elements of prayer found in this passage. Do you use these elements in your own prayer life? Explain.

- Read Mark 12:29–31. How do these commands summarise all the Bible's teaching? How do they fit together?

CHAPTER 6   GOD'S CHRISTMAS CARDS

Points to Ponder

'If our greatest need had been information, God would have sent an educator. If our greatest need had been technology, God would have sent us a scientist. If our greatest need had been money, God would have sent us an economist. But since our greatest need was forgiveness, God sent us a Saviour.'

1   Do you agree that our greatest need was forgiveness?

2   Explain why you think this is true.

'He became like us, so we could become like Him.'

1   In what way did He become like us?

2   In what way can we become like Him?

Wisdom from the Word

🦋 Read Matthew 1:18–2:12. If you were to write a commercial Christmas-card message based on this passage, what element of the story would you highlight? Why?

🦋 Read Luke 2:1–20. If you were to write a commercial Christmas-card message based on this passage, what element of the story would you highlight? Why?

CHAPTER 7   BEHIND THE SHOWER CURTAIN

Points to Ponder

'I've never been surprised by God's judgement, but I'm still stunned by His grace.'

1   Have you ever been surprised by God's judgement? By His grace? Explain.

2   Why is grace usually more of a surprise to us than judgement?

'Seems that God is looking more for ways to get us home than for ways to keep us out. I challenge you to find one soul who came to God seeking grace and did not find it.'

1   What ways did God use to get you 'home"?

2   Accept Max's challenge—can you think of one biblical person who sought God's grace but didn't find it? How significant is this? Why?

'I'm not for watering-down the truth or compromising the gospel. But if a fellow with a pure heart calls God, *Father*, can't I call that same man, *Brother*? If God doesn't make doctrinal perfection a requirement for family membership, should I?'

1   What do you think Max means by 'a fellow with a pure heart'?

2   What would happen if 'doctrinal perfection' were made 'a requirement for family membership'?

Wisdom from the Word

❦   Read Luke 19:1–10. How did grace change Zacchaeus? Do you think he was surprised by grace? How about those around him? Explain.

❦   Read Luke 15:3–7. To whom did Jesus direct this parable? Why is that significant? What was His main point? What do you learn about grace from this parable?

∞

CHAPTER 8   GABRIEL'S QUESTIONS

Points to Ponder

'Are we still stunned by God's coming? Still staggered by the event? Does Christmas still spawn the same speechless wonder it did two thousand years ago?'

1   Are you 'still stunned by God's coming"?

2   How do you stay ready to allow God to stun you?

> 'Why is it that out of a hundred or so of God's chil-
> dren only two paused to consider His Son? What is
> this December demon that steals our eyes and stills
> our tongues? Isn't this the season to pause and pose
> Gabriel's questions? The tragedy is not that I can't
> answer them, but that I am too busy to ask them.'

1   How do you explain 'this December demon that steals
    our eyes and stills our tongues"?

2   Which of Gabriel's questions most intrigue you? Why?

Wisdom from the Word

- Read Luke 1:5–20; 26–38. Compare verse 18 with verse
  34. Why do you think Gabriel reacted so differently to
  these questions? Do you think Gabriel was a very gra-
  cious 'personality"? Explain.

- Read Daniel 8:15–19; 9:20–22. What do you learn about
  Gabriel's personality from these passages? If he were to
  appear to you, how do you think you'd respond?

CHAPTER 9   WHAT IS YOUR PRICE?

Points to Ponder

> "Take your pick. Just choose one option and the money
> is yours.' A deep voice from another microphone begins
> reading the list: "Put your children up for adoption;
> become a prostitute for a week; give up citizenship of

your country; abandon your church; abandon your family; kill a stranger; have a sex-change operation; leave your spouse; change your race." "That's the list," the host proclaims. "Now make your choice." '

1   If you were a contestant on this show, how would you respond?

2   What is your price?

'A schoolboy was once asked to define the parts of speech *I* and *mine*. He answered "aggressive pronouns." '

1   What is the problem with 'aggressive pronouns'?

2   What is the cost of selfishness?

Wisdom from the Word

🌹 Read Luke 12:13–21. What point about greed does Jesus make in this passage? What is His main point?

🌹 Read Deuteronomy 10:14–15. According to this passage, why does greed make no sense? What is the connection between verses 14 and 15?

🌹 Read Hebrews 13:5–6. What negative command is given here? What positive command? What reason is given for obeying the commands? What results from obeying the commands?

CHAPTER 10   GROCERIES AND GRACE

Points to Ponder

'We, too, have been graced with a surprise. Even more than that of the lady. For though her debt was high, she could pay it. We can't begin to pay ours. We, like the woman, have been given a gift. Not just at the checkout stand, but at the judgement seat. And we, too, have become a bride. Not just for a moment, but for eternity. And not just for groceries, but for the feast.'

1   In what way have we been 'graced with a surprise'?

2   Why can't we begin to pay our debt?

3   What gift will we be given at the judgement seat?

4   In what way have we become a bride?

5   What is the feast Max mentions?

6   Do you expect to be at the feast? Explain.

Wisdom from the Word

❧   Read Romans 5:6–11. For whom did Christ die (v. 6)? Why is this an example of grace? What is the result of embracing grace (v. 11)? Is this characteristic of your experience? Explain.

❧   Read Revelation 19:6–9. What is the mood of the event described in this passage? Who are the main participants? Do you expect to be there? Why or why not?

CHAPTER 11   THE CHOICE

Points to Ponder

'Love, joy, peace, patience, kindness, goodness, faithfulness, gentleness, and self-control. To these I commit my day. If I succeed, I will give thanks. If I fail, I will seek His grace. And then, when this day is done, I will place my head on my pillow and rest. I choose God.'

1   What do you think of the philosophy of life expressed in the paragraph above? Does it work? Explain.

2   What does Max mean, 'I choose God.' How do you *choose* God?

Wisdom from the Word

🍇   Read Galatians 5:22–23. Why is there no law against the things listed in this passage? To what are these things compared in verses 19–21? Which list do you find yourself in most often?

🍇   Read Deuteronomy 30:19–20 and Joshua 24:14–15. What choices are we given in these two passages? In what way are these choices the same ones we must make? What choice have you made? Explain.

CHAPTER 12   THE PROPHET

Points to Ponder

'One dresses like Jesus, but the other acts like Jesus. One introduced himself as an ambassador for Christ, the other didn't have to. One stirred my curiosity, but the other touched my heart.'

1   Which of these two men would you most like to meet? Explain.

2   Which of these two men would you most like to spend a week with? Explain.

'Something told me that if Jesus were here, in person, in San Antonio and I ran into Him in a grocery store, I wouldn't recognize Him by His rake, robe, and big Bible. But I would know Him for His good heart and kind words.'

1   How do you think Jesus would dress if He walked the streets of our world today? Could you pick Him out of a crowd? Explain.

2   How do you think He would act?

Wisdom from the Word

🌾   Read 1 John 2:3–6. How can we know that we have come to know Jesus (v. 3)? What happens to someone who obeys God's Word (v. 5)? If we claim to know Jesus, what are we to do (v. 6)?

🌾   Read Luke 6:43–45. How can you tell a bad 'tree' from a good one? What sort of 'fruit' would others say you bear?

🌾   Read Ephesians 5:1–2. What commands are we given in this passage? What example are we given?

CHAPTER 13   WHEN CRICKETS MAKE YOU CRANKY

Points to Ponder

'When we are mistreated, our animalistic response is to go on the hunt. Instinctively we double up our fists. Getting even is only natural. Which, incidentally, is precisely the problem. Revenge is natural, not spiritual. Getting even is the rule of the jungle. Giving grace is the rule of the kingdom.'

1   Does the 'rule of the jungle' or the 'rule of the kingdom' most often characterise your response to mistreatment?

2   Give an example of how you react to mistreatment.

'Revenge is irreverent. When we strike back we are saying, "I know vengeance is yours, God, but I just didn't think you'd punish enough. I thought I'd better take this situation into my own hands. You have a tendency to be a little soft." '

1   Have you ever felt the way the paragraph above describes? Explain.

2   If you've ever acted out this feeling, what was the result?

'Forgiveness comes easier with a wide-angle lens. Joseph uses one to get the whole picture. He refuses to focus on the betrayal of his brothers without also seeing the loyalty of his God.'

1   How does forgiveness come easier with a 'wide-angle lens'?

2   How is it made more difficult with a 'telephoto lens'?

Wisdom from the Word

🌱   Read Proverbs 20:22. What negative command is given here? What positive command is given? How do the two work together?

🌱   Read Genesis 50:15-21. Did Joseph have a right to be angry about the way his brothers mistreated him? How did he react? What was the result? If you were Joseph, how do you think you would have reacted?

∞

CHAPTER 14   SEEING WHAT EYES CAN'T

Points to Ponder

'There is more to life than meets the eye. For that's what faith is. Faith is trusting what the eye can't see. Eyes see the prowling lion. Faith sees Daniel's angel. Eyes see storms. Faith sees Noah's rainbow. Eyes see giants. Faith sees Canaan.'

1   Do you agree that 'faith is trusting what the eye can't see'?

2   Is there more to it than that? Explain.

"I only jump to big arms." If we think the arms are weak, we won't jump. For that reason, the Father flexed His muscles.'

1   How has God demonstrated His 'big arms' in your own life?

2   What's the biggest 'arm flexing' you've ever experienced?

Wisdom from the Word

☙   Read Hebrews 11:1–3. How is faith defined in this passage? How would you put this in your own words?

☙   Read Psalm 20. What lessons of trust do you learn from this passage? What promises are given? What hope is expressed?

☙   Read Ephesians 1:19–20. Does this passage help build your own faith? Explain. How does Paul use this passage in Ephesians?

∞

204 When God Whispers Your Name

CHAPTER 15 OVERCOMING YOUR HERITAGE

Points to Ponder

'We can't choose our parents, but we can choose our mentors.'

1   What mentors have you chosen?

2   Why did you choose these particular individuals?

'Maybe your past isn't much to brag about. You saw raw evil. And now you, like Josiah, have to make a choice. Do you rise above the past and make a difference? Or do you remain controlled by the past and make excuses?'

1   Choose one word to describe how you feel about your past: Grateful? Angry? Discouraged? Proud? Depressed? Blessed?

2   How do we sometimes allow ourselves to be controlled by the past? Have you ever slipped into this mode? Explain.

'Spiritual life comes from the Spirit! Your parents may have given you genes, but God gives you grace. Your parents may be responsible for your body, but God has taken charge of your soul. You may get your looks from your mother, but you get eternity from your Father, your heavenly Father.'

1   How does this principle change our whole outlook?

2   What sort of spiritual heritage do you have now? Describe it.

Wisdom from the Word

❦   Read 2 Kings 21. Describe Josiah's heritage. How do you think he felt about it?

❦ Read John 3:1–8. How did Jesus explain that we can receive a spiritual heritage? What must we do? How did the Spirit move in your own life? Where did the 'wind' come from?

❦ Read 2 Corinthians 5:17. What does it mean to be 'in Christ'? What is gained? What is lost?

CHAPTER 16 THE SWEET SOUND OF THE SECOND FIDDLE

Points to Ponder

'You've been playing second fiddle for too long. You need to step out on your own.'

1   Have you ever received advice like the statement above?

2   Have you ever given such advice? What was the result of acting on such advice?

'Living off the praise of others is an erratic diet.'

1   What does the statement above mean?

2   In what way is it an 'erratic diet'?

'To this day whenever the sun shines and the moon reflects and the darkness is illuminated, the moon doesn't complain or get jealous. He does what he was intended to do all along; the moon beams.'

1   What is the result of doing what you were created to do?

2   Do you know this feeling? Explain.

Wisdom from the Word

🌳   Read 1 Corinthians 12:12–30. How could heeding the advice in this passage have saved the moon from a lot of grief? Is there a lesson here for you? If so, what is it?

🌳   Read Romans 12:3–8. How could the advice given in verse 3 have spared the moon some pain? How does it fit in with the guidelines laid out in the rest of the passage?

🌳   Read Isaiah 43:5–7. For what were we created, according to Isaiah? How do we 'glorify" God? Are you doing so? Explain.

CHAPTER 17   YOUR SACK OF STONES

Points to Ponder

'Could it be that you went to religion and didn't go to God? Could it be that you went to a church, but never saw Christ?'

1   Have you ever gone to 'religion" instead of God? If so, what happened?

2   How is it possible to go to church but not see Christ? Do you see Christ when you go to church? Explain.

'Go to Him. Be honest with Him. Admit you have soul secrets you've never dealt with. He already knows what they are. He's just waiting for you to ask Him to help. He's just waiting for you to give Him your sack. Go ahead. You'll be glad you did.'

1   How do you go to Jesus? Have you ever gone to Him like this?

2   Ask yourself what things are in your sack. Have you brought these things to Him? If not, why not?

Wisdom from the Word

🍇   Read 2 Corinthians 7:5–13. What is the connection between sorrow and regret in this passage (see especially verse 10)? What does godly sorrow produce?

🍇   Read Matthew 11:28–30. What does Jesus tell us to do in this passage? How do we do it? What is the result? Have you experienced such 'rest'? Explain.

CHAPTER 18   OF OZ AND GOD

Points to Ponder

'   "The power you need is really a power you already have. Just look deep enough, long enough, and there's nothing you can't do."Sound familiar? Sound patriotic? Sound . . . Christian?'

1   When was the last time you heard a statement similar to the one quoted above? Describe it.

2   Was there ever a time such statements sounded Christian to you? Explain.

'Do-it-yourself Christianity is not much encouragement to the done-in and worn-out.'

1   What does Max mean by 'do-it-yourself Christianity'?

2   Why is such Christianity not much encouragement to the 'done-in and worn-out'?

'The wizard says look inside yourself and find self. God says look inside yourself and find God. The first will get you to Kansas. The latter will get you to heaven. Take your pick.'

1　How could Max's phrase 'look inside yourself and find God' be misunderstood?

2　How do you think it should be understood?

Wisdom from the Word

☙　Read Matthew 19:17. What was Jesus' point in telling the young man this statement? What did He want him to understand? Did the young man 'get it'? Explain.

☙　Read 1 Corinthians 6:9–11. What lie did Paul not want the Corinthians to believe? How had their lives radically changed? Who caused the change?

☙　Read Romans 1:17. Where does 'righteousness' come from, according to this verse? What does faith have to do with it? How is this different from the wizard's message?

∞

CHAPTER 19　AN INSIDE JOB

Points to Ponder

'You can't fix an inside problem by going outside.'

1　What 'inside problem' is Max talking about?

2　Why can't you fix it from the 'outside'?

'Society may renovate, but only God re-creates.'

1   Why can't society re-create?

2   Why doesn't God merely renovate?

'The next time alarms go off in your world, ask yourself three questions: (1) Is there any unconfessed sin in
my life? (2) Are there any unresolved conflicts in my
world? (3) Are there any unsurrendered worries in my
heart?'

1   Ask yourself the questions Max lists above.

2   What answers do you come up with? What do you need
to do, if anything?

Wisdom from the Word

❦   Read Psalm 32:1–5. How did David at first deal with his
own sin? What happened? How did he then respond?
What happened?

❦   Read Psalm 51:10. How is this a prayer for every believer
in every age? Is this a part of your own prayer life? Explain.

❦   Read 1 Peter 5:7. What command is given? What reason
is given for the command? How can we follow this
command in a practical sense?

∞

CHAPTER 20   LATE-NIGHT GOOD NEWS

Points to Ponder

'Does someone have a hand on the throttle of this train
or has the engineer bailed out just as we come in sight of
dead-man's curve?'

1   Have you ever asked yourself a question like the one above?

2   If so, what were the circumstances?

'The promise of the Messiah threads its way through forty-two generations of rough-cut stones, forming a necklace fit for the King who came. Just as promised.'

1   Are you surprised at the ancestors in the Messiah's family tree? Why or why not?

2   Why is this genealogy 'fit for the King who came'?

3   Why do you think God chose to record His family tree?

'The engineer has not abandoned the train. Nuclear war is no threat to God. Yo-yo economies don't intimidate the heavens. Immoral leaders have never derailed the plan. God keeps His promise.'

1   How can a firm belief in the truth expressed above keep our heads above water?

2   What evidence in your own world do you see of its truth?

3   What biblical evidence can you cite?

Wisdom from the Word

❧   Read John 16:33. What promise does Jesus give us in this passage? What warning does He give? What does it mean to 'take heart'? Why should we take heart?

❧   Read Daniel 4:34–35. What lesson did Nebuchadnezzar learn about God's control of the universe? How did this lesson affect him?

❧   Read Isaiah 43:11–13. What does God Himself say about His control of the universe? What phrase in this passage is most memorable for you? Why?

∞

CHAPTER 21   HEALTHY HABITS

Points to Ponder

'Pick a time in the not-too-distant past. A year or two ago. Now ask yourself a few questions. How does your prayer life today compare with then? How about your giving? Have both the amount and the joy increased? What about your church loyalty? Can they tell you've grown? And Bible study? Are you learning to learn?'

1   Ask yourself the questions Max lists above.

2   How are you doing in these areas?

'Growth is the goal of the Christian. Maturity is mandatory.'

1   In what way is growth the goal of the Christian?

2   How is maturity mandatory?

'There they are: prayer, study, giving, fellowship. Four habits worth having. Isn't it good to know that some habits are good for you? Make them a part of your day and grow. Don't make the mistake of the little boy. Don't stay too close to where you got in. It's risky resting on the edge.'

1   Evaluate yourself in your performance of each of the four habits Max lists.

2   Which are your strengths? Your weaknesses?

3   What can you do to improve?

Wisdom from the Word

🍇   Read Colossians 1:9–12. What specific requests did Paul make for the Colossians? How can these requests help shape our own prayer life?

🍁 Read 1 Peter 2:2–3. What command are we given here? What result is promised? What motivation is given?

🍁 Read 2 Peter 3:18. What does it mean to grow in grace? What does it mean to grow in knowledge? How are the two related?

∞

CHAPTER 22 DFW AND THE HOLY SPIRIT

Points to Ponder

'No matter how you travel, the trip can get tiring. Wouldn't it be great to discover a people-mover for your heart?'

1 What does Max mean by a 'people-mover for your heart'?

2 Would you want one? Explain.

'The next time you need to rest, go ahead. He'll keep you headed in the right direction. And the next time you make progress—thank Him. He's the one providing the power. And the next time you want to give up? Don't. Please don't. Turn the next corner. You may be surprised at what you find. Besides, you've got a flight home you don't want to miss.'

1 How does the Holy Spirit accomplish each of the things Max lists above? Have you experienced these things in your own life? Explain.

2 What is this 'flight home' Max writes about? How do you book reservations for it?

Wisdom from the Word

 ❦ Read Colossians 1:28–29. What was Paul's goal for his ministry? What did it take to accomplish this goal? Is this any different for us? Explain.

 ❦ Read Hebrews 10:32–36. How does the writer encourage his readers to not give up? What reasons does he give? What promise does he give? What warning does he give?

CHAPTER 23   THE GOD WHO FIGHTS FOR YOU

Points to Ponder

'If you don't know what to do, it's best just to sit tight till God does His thing.'

1   What do you think of this advice?

2   Is this hard for you to act on? Explain.

'If some guy has you on the ground pounding on you and your father is within earshot and tells you to call him anytime you need help, what would you do? I'd call my father. That's all I do. When the battle is too great, I ask God to take over. I get the Father to fight for me.'

1   How do we get the Father to fight for us in our day-to-day lives?

2   What does this mean? What can we expect?

'His job is to fight. Our job is to trust. Just trust. Not direct. Or question. Or yank the steering wheel out of

His hands. Our job is to pray and wait. Nothing more is necessary. Nothing more is needed.'

1   What does it mean for you personally to 'trust'?

2   What is the relationship between acting in faith and waiting in prayer?

Wisdom from the Word

❦   Read Exodus 14. In what ways did Moses trust God in this chapter? In what ways did God fight for him? What was the result?

❦   Read 2 Chronicles 20:1–30. In what ways did Jehoshaphat trust God in this passage? In what ways did God fight for him? What was the result? How do you respond to the king's statement in verse 12b?

❦   Read Psalm 115. What difficulties were the people facing at this time? How did they respond? What did God do? How can their example help us?

∞

CHAPTER 24   THE GIFT OF UNHAPPINESS

Points to Ponder

'Unhappiness on earth cultivates a hunger for heaven. By gracing us with a deep dissatisfaction, God holds our attention. The only tragedy, then, is to be satisfied prematurely. To settle for earth. To be content in a strange land. To intermarry with the Babylonians and forget Jerusalem.'

1   In what way can dissatisfaction be called an example of grace?

2   What does it mean to 'intermarry with the Babylonians and forget Jerusalem'? Are you ever tempted to do this? Explain.

'You will never be completely happy on earth simply because you were not made for earth. Oh, you will have your moments of joy. You will catch glimpses of light. You will know moments or even days of peace. But they simply do not compare with the happiness that lies ahead.'

1   Why does Max say we were not made for earth?

2   What would be the problem with becoming completely happy on earth?

'Lower your expectations of earth. This is not heaven, so don't expect it to be. There will never be a news bulletin with no bad news. There will never be a church with no gossip or competition. There will never be a new car, new wife, or new baby who can give you the joy your heart craves. Only God can.'

1   How can we practically lower our expectations of earth?

2   Give several examples.

Wisdom from the Word

❧   Read Ecclesiastes 3:11. What does it mean to say that 'he set eternity in the hearts of men?' How does this reveal itself?

❧   Read 1 Peter 2:11. How does an 'alien' or a 'stranger in the world' live differently than natives? How do sinful desires war against the soul? How does living like an alien help in this battle?

❧   Read 1 Corinthians 2:9–10. Why is this probably the

best picture of heaven we can understand? Does this passage give you hope? Explain.

CHAPTER 25   ON SEEING GOD

Points to Ponder

'Who wants heaven without God? Heaven is not heaven without God.'

1   Why would heaven cease to be heaven without God?

2   Would you want to live in such a place? Explain.

'Contentment is a difficult virtue. Why? Because there is nothing on earth that can satisfy our deepest longing. We long to see God. The leaves of life are rustling with the rumour that we will—and we won't be satisfied until we do.'

1   Do you agree with Max's explanation for why contentment is hard to achieve?

2   Are there any other reasons it may be hard to achieve? Explain.

'Upon seeing God, Isaiah was terrified. Why such fear? Why did he tremble so? Because he was wax before the sun. A candle in a hurricane. A minnow at Niagara. God's glory was too great. His purity too sterling. His power too mighty. The holiness of God illuminates the sinfulness of man.'

1   Define God's holiness.

2   Why should it terrify Isaiah?

Wisdom from the Word

- Read Exodus 33:12–23. Would you have made Moses' request recorded in verse 18? What does it mean that he could not see God's 'face'? How does this relate to God's holiness?

- Read Isaiah 6:1–7; Hebrews 12:14; Revelation 1:12–18. How do people normally respond to God's unveiled holiness? Why is this so? What does this suggest about the way we should relate to God?

- Read Psalm 17:15. What will finally satisfy us, according to David? Why should this satisfy us?

∞

CHAPTER 26   ORPHANS AT THE GATE

Points to Ponder

'Earth is not what we'd hoped. It may have its moments, but it is simply not what we think it should be. Something inside us groans for more.'

1   In what ways is earth not what you'd hoped for?

2   Do you 'groan" for something more? Explain.

'We are so eager we demand. We demand in this world what only the next world can give. No sickness. No suffering. No struggle. We stomp our feet and shake our fists, forgetting it is only in heaven that such peace is found.'

1   Do you ever find yourself demanding what properly belongs to the next world?

2   If so, what causes this? What is the result?

Wisdom from the Word

🌰 Read Romans 8:18–25. How does the hope of 'redemption' make life easier in our 'groaning'? How does this groaning display itself? What ultimate hope do we have?

🌰 Read 2 Corinthians 5:1–10. For what purpose did God make us (vs. 4–5)? Where does living by faith come in (v. 7)? What is our goal in the meanwhile (v. 9)? What motivation is given (v. 10)?

CHAPTER 27   VIEW OF THE HIGH COUNTRY

Points to Ponder

'All of us need help sometimes. This journey gets steep. So steep that some of us give up.'

1   Are you ever tempted to give up?

2   What circumstances prompt this urge?

'The human blood of the divine Christ covers our sins and proclaims a message: *We have been bought. We cannot be sold. Ever.*'

1   How does the statement above make you feel?

2   Explain why.

'Believe me when I say it will be worth it. No cost is too high. If you must pay a price, pay it! No sacrifice is too much. If you must leave baggage on the trail, leave it! No loss will compare. Whatever it takes, do it.'

1   What price might you be asked to pay in your own life? What sacrifices might you have to make?

2   What 'baggage' do you need to 'leave on the trail'? What baggage can you help others leave?

Wisdom from the Word

❧   Read Hebrews 12:22–24. How is our future described in this passage? What picture do you get of it? Does this encourage you? If so, how? If not, why not?

❧   Read 1 Corinthians 6:19–20. To whom do you belong, according to this passage? How did this happen? How are we to respond?

❧   Read Romans 8:35–39. Are any possible enemies left off this list? How certain is our destiny? How is this destiny made certain? How does this make you feel? Why?

∞

CHAPTER 28   THE NAME ONLY GOD KNOWS

Points to Ponder

'Isn't it incredible to think that God has saved a name just for you? One you don't even know? We've always assumed that the name we got is the name we will keep. Apparently your future is so promising that it warrants a new title. Your eternity is so special, no common name will do.'

1   Have you ever had a 'secret name'? Have you ever given anyone else one? If so, what was the purpose of these names? How did they make the recipient feel?

2   If you were to be given a 'secret name' based on a charac-

ter trait, what trait would you most want to be known for?

'There is more to your life than you ever thought. There is more to your story than what you have read. There is more to your song than what you have sung. A good author saves the best for last. A great composer keeps his finest for the finish. And God, the author of life and composer of hope, has done the same for you.'

1   Is it easy for you to believe that 'there is more to your life than you ever thought?' Explain.

2   What are you most looking forward in the world to come? Describe it.

Wisdom from the Word

❧   Read Isaiah 56:3–5. What problems did God address in these verses? What were the people tempted to think? Have you ever thought this way? If so, explain. What does God promise in verse 5?

❧   Read Revelation 2:17. What does it mean to be an 'overcomer'? What is promised such a person? Do you hope to be such a person? Explain.

❧   Read Zephaniah 3:17. What role does God play in this verse? What is the mood of this verse? Does this verse give you something to look forward to? Does it encourage you? Explain.